GULSIFAT SHAKHIDI

TRUE PARADISE
LOST PARADISE

SELECTED ARTICLES, REVIEWS AND INTERVIEWS

Hertfordshire Press Ltd © 2019
e-mail: publisher@hertfordshirepress.com
www.hertfordshirepress.com

On behalf of Eurasian Creative Guild, London

TRUE PARADISE - LOST PARADISE

Selected Articles, Reviews And Interviews
by Gulsifat Shakhidi ©

English / Russian

Edited by Vera Deinichenko (Russian)
Stephen M. Bland (English)
Translated by Tatiana Kinzhalova

---

*British Library Catalogue in Publication Data
A catalogue record for this book is available from the British Library
Library of Congress in Publication Data
A catalogue record for this book has been requested*

ISBN: 978-1-913356-02-6

СОДЕРЖАНИЕ

TICK MARKS TO THE PORTRAIT

True Paradise - Lost Paradise is a collection of journalistic pieces written by Gulsifat Shahidi, the prolific author and Laureate of the Eurasian Creative Guild. This was the tenth book by my friend and countrywoman to be published by the Moscow-based Publishing House, Pen.

For both of us, 'Lost Paradise' is the best city in the world, Dushanbe, the capital of incomparable Tajikistan. The new book by Gulsifat Shahidi presents the author's reminiscences about her youth, her first steps in journalism with the youth newspaper, *Komsomolets Tajikistana*, and her creative efforts to master the skills of essay writing, interviews and reviews. This collection comes from a period when we were both looking for our own style of narrative writing, believing sincerely that each person we meet in our path through life is unique, interesting, and will teach us many things.

I have entitled my introduction to this collection 'Tick Marks to the Portrait' because the reader will see how Gulsifat draws a portrait of our generation, and, by extension, a portrait of our native Tajikistan, ticking the boxes of various genres as her writing progressed. One should pay special attention to how keen and exciting the questions which the author-journalist puts to her countrymen are, and how sincere the answers of her conversation partners. As a professional writer, I assure you that a partner in conversation is not ready to open his or her soul and tell their innermost thoughts to every journalist. Gulsifat forms the basis of her interviews on a mutual trust. Collected in this volume are the author's interviews with some of her heroes: Gulchehra Sharipova, a politician and State Counsellor of Justice ('A Woman of Strong Character'), Gennady Ratushenko, a photo-artist, patriot and promoter of Tajikistan culture worldwide ('A Photo is a Visual Memory of History'), Zarrina Mirshakar, the first and only female composer in the Pamir Region ('A Prelude to Nowruz'), and the monumental artist, Murivat Beknazarov ('I am a Highlander, and That Says it All'). These interviews, published in the newspaper *Vechorka* between 1999 and 2006, continue to strike the imagination with the power of their characters and their creative ideas.

The fratricidal Civil War of the 1990s scattered the Tajik people to all parts of the globe. Gulsifat has been living in two cities - Moscow and London - for almost twenty-five years now. Whilst in London it occurred to her to collect her published journalistic work and TV transmissions made during her time at the Tajik daughter company of MGRTK (MIR) into one volume. We both cried bitter tears when we worked on the book, *The City Where Dreams Come True*, Gulsifat, as its author suffering once again upon recollecting the terrifying events of the war, and me as its editor feeling the pain inherent in the confrontation between different political groups during those years. Published in London

in 2005, it won the main prize at a festival dedicated to international literature, and Gulsifat was awarded the Gold Medal: 'A Dove of Peace.'

During the five years of our collaboration with the Moscow Publishing House, Pen, the following books by Gulsifat have been published: a collection of short stories entitled *My Neighbourhood Sisters*, the novella *Farhod from Navgilem*, an autobiographical book about family *Share Love*, an academic book about Vasily Zhukovsky's creative translations *I am Looking Towards the East*, a book on the mutual influence of Russian and Tajik literature of the 1920-30s *A Sentimental Journey*, a novel *My Light, Honey*, a book for children *Tales of Grandma Gulsifat*, a selection of collected works *In this Corner of the Earth*, and the collected journalistic works, *True Paradise - Lost Paradise*. I present the last of these titles to the reader.

Gulsifat has collected the articles written in the years which followed perestroika (the period of reformation) into a separate part. The author expresses her unceasing concern about the preservation of national traditions and the purity of the native language ('The Great Men of the Tajik People,' 'No Matter Where You Come From, It Matters Who You Are'). The articles 'True Paradise - Lost Paradise,' 'Time Contrasts,' and 'How Wonderful it is to Live, How Badly We are Living…' are filled with reasoning about nostalgia and its consequences. Gulsifat substantiates her thoughts by reciting lines from classics by figures such as Jalāl ad-Dīn Rumi, Marcel Proust, Friedrich Nietzsche, Boris Slutsky and Marina Tsvetaeva.

The selection of travel essays were written by Gulsifat following presentations of her books in various countries. It transpires that Shahidi's characters are understood and empathised with by people irrespective of their location, age or nationality. This discovery left a strong impression on the author in New York and Washington ('So Near and So Far Away, America), in Tel-Aviv and Jerusalem ('Reflections at the Temple of the Holy Sepulchre'), in Lerice, Pisa and Florence ('Italy: The Bay of Poets and a New Centre of High Arts'), and in the provincial city of Suvorov in the Tula Region of Russia ('A New Meeting in Zhukovsky's Homeland').

Gulsifat Shahidi is a member of the Union of Writers of Russia and sits on the Executive and Consulting Council of the Eurasian Creative Guild. In London, she became acquainted with many interesting writers and poets who compose their creations in Russian. She considers it both useful and beneficial to take the creative works of her contemporaries very much to heart. She is charmed by the images and ideas of Dilyara Lindsay ('I Learnt to Trust the Sound') and reviews the book *Curls of Karakuls* by Kazakh writer, Raushan Burkitaeva-Nurkenova ('A Jug of Feminine Melodies by Raushan'). In her review of *Amina Turan in the Country of Nomads* by Zaure Turekhanova, Gulsifat sees similarities with *Alice's Adventures in Wonderland* and admires the beauty of mythological epic literature and Kazakh folklore. Her heart was also touched by the poems by Abu-Sufyan, a poet from Dagestan whose book, *Crane* she reviews with glowing praise.

I was with Gulsifat in Moscow for the presentation of a book by Megan Werner, a writer from South Africa, *It's Up to Me: Seven Ways to Make a Difference*. Megan was very young, still a teenager, but she struck both of us with her views on life. She was very thankful to Gulsifat for her review of the book ('Bravo, Megan! Or an Old Head on Young Shoulders').

I would like to place particular emphasis on the reviews of works by our friends and countrymen. Gulsifat's review of *Films by Bako Sadykov* ('That's All. There will be No Movie') is an example of lines written with a heavy heart. As great admirers of classic Tajik movies, for both of us the loss of this genre is painful. We both knew Sadykov, our 'Tajik Tarkovsky' and founder of the Tajik poetic movie whose films won prestigious prices at international festivals well. Nowadays, the master lives in the wilderness in Uzbekistan, and his unique films have not been preserved. The director's best friend, Makhmudov has collected unique documents, letters to the Goskino Organisation, personal letters, photos and film scenarios into a single tome. Gulsifat comments on the book with reference to the principles of Sufism and immortal eastern poetry.

The book written by Gulsifat's colleague, the journalist Umed Babakhanov is called *The Tajiks are Coming*, and Gulsifat kept the same title for her review. In it she expresses her excitement at the author's honesty and bravery as a military journalist.

The novel *Zahhak* by our friend and countrymen, Vladimir Medvedev - which became a sensation in Moscow

- is not overlooked by Shahidi. Medvedev grew up in Tajik-istan and knows its culture, language and ancient folk liter-ature well. During the Civil War of the 90s, he met with the representatives of different political groups and interviewed commanders, troops and bandits alike. Terrifying 'Zahhak' is a mythological character, a symbiosis of a human and a reptile from Ferdowsi's epic poem, *Shahnameh*. Gulsifat en-titled her review of that novel, 'If Only There was no War.' It is the sacred desire of all mothers in the world to live in peace and to prevent bloodshed in their native lands. It is this desire which drives Gulsifat to write.

In this collection there is also a sprinkling of joy among the various genres in the way of a sketch, a humoresque en-titled 'A Medical Treatment Room.' Have you already passed your health assessment test, my dear readers? If not, then two pensioners will show you to do it correctly. Let's read and laugh together.

Vera Deinichenko, Journalist

ARTICLES

THE GREAT MEN OF THE TAJIK PEOPLE

Since ancient times there has been a tradition amongst the Tajik people: when a child is born, a handwritten volume of the wisdom of the centuries, the original text of the Quran or the book of ghazals by Hafiz, who recited the Quran in verse, is placed under the child's pillow. It is believed that this will help a child to grow up to be wise and inspired in their creative activity.

Such belief in the power of a written source is no accident. Not many places can be found on this Earth where so many great scientists, poets, talented artists and architects were born. Their names could occupy many pages, but a few will serve to give an idea. In the field of science, there are Avicenna, Al-Khwarizmi, Al-Farabi and Al-Biruni. In literature, there are such first-rate stars (according to Goethe) as Rudaki, Ferdowsi, Khayyam, Rumi, Saadi, Hafiz and Jami. The masters of art, Borbad, Mani and Behzod are known far beyond the bounds of ancient Sogdiana, the state of the Samanids and Mavrennakhr (Transoxiana) - the main territories which constitute modern Central Asia. One can argue about the details in the biography of each of these figures, but one fact remains indisputable: the native language of these and many other classics was Persian.

The ancient wisdom of the East has served as the basis for the development of many areas in natural sciences and philosophy. Three pillars of science are well known: Al-Khwarizmi (8th-9th c.), who discovered the fundamental canons of arithmetic and algebra and had a great influence on the development of mathematics in Western Europe; Al-Biruni (10th-11th c.), the philosopher who commented on Aristotle and was given the name, the Second Teacher (i.e. the second after Aristotle); and, of course, Avicenna, who considered himself a student and successor to the great scholars of the West and the East and was so because he summed up and then developed the experience of Greek, ancient Roman, Indian and Asian scientists in his book, *A Canon of Medicine*.

Medieval Europe became acquainted with that masterpiece of medical science in the 13th century as soon as it was translated into Latin. For more than five-hundred-years it served as a theoretical and practical guide for European doctors. The acute need for the book, *A Canon of Medicine* was the reason that it was republished multiple times. The belles-letters and philosophical writings of Avicenna had a great influence on the subsequent development of literature in both the East and the West. Motifs from his belles-letters and philosophical narratives can even be seen in *The Divine Comedy* by Dante, who mentioned his being an outstanding thinker.

Omar Khayyam is known in Europe as a poet - the master of quatrains, a jovial free-thinker, the laconic poems by whom combine depth, elegance of form and rare wit with an astonishing zest for life. Not everyone knows, however, that Omar Khayyam was first and foremost an outstanding astronomer and a mathematician, the architect of a mathematical discovery which was found later in the West and named Newton's binomial. An author unsurpassed in accuracy even in our time, the wise philosopher Khayyam was the true successor to Aristotle.

Poetic words were not only a way of expressing one's inspirational thoughts and concentrating the age-old wisdom of the people for Oriental masters of the pen, they were also an important means of educating people and influencing powerful men. Rudaki (9th-10th c.), for example, was not only a poet, the founder of Tajik-Persian literature, but also a tutor referred to respectfully as an '*ustod*' (a teacher). So he remains today. The poets of the East were mentors not only in terms of their creative activity. The great Sufi poet and philosopher, Jalāl ad-Dīn Rumi (13th c.) raised and educated his son, the prolific poet, Sultan Walad. In addition to being a bard, philosopher, philologist and a musicologist, the wise and sedate Jami (15th c.) also became a teacher and a mentor to Alisher Navoiy, the founder of modern Turkish literature.

Goethe greatly appreciated Tajik-Persian poetry. Being inspired by it, he created a book of verses, *West-Eastern Divan* (the Persian name for a collection of poems). This work had a great influence on European literature and heightened interest in Eastern poetry. That became possible because Ta-

jik-Persian poetry is not simply literature but also a source of wisdom and knowledge. It is a textbook for life in which everyone can find something valuable which is to be cherished. In order to do this, one simply needs - according to the words of Pushkin - to truly understand the 'truth of the ancient East.'

NO MATTER WHERE YOU COME FROM, IT MATTERS WHO YOU ARE

There is probably no other language in the world in which there are so many local idioms, dialects and parlances. For example, when I arrive on a trip to my beloved Dushanbe, many of my friends meet me and everyone inquires: '*Chi kheli? Chitu shumo? Tinji?*' etc. All of this means just one thing: 'how are you' or 'how do you feel?' As one dialect currently dominates, now being comprehensible to everyone, one might be excused for thinking that people have begun to speak in a manner closer to the literary language. But no, in everyday conversation young people use mostly southern dialects in the streets.

This is how my city greets me every time, with a variety of vernaculars in addition to a multitude of changes and the multicolour brilliance of its uniqueness. As a warm summer breeze spreads the petals of mountain flowers across the globe, in the same way, many of us have been scattered around the globe from our Tajik homeland. Many of us currently live in different parts of the world and unite into diasporas; but everyone looks forward to meeting once again

with their native land.

Each time, when passing along the main avenue of the city, one notices how the city has been transformed. Everything is changing, but my favourite middle alley pleases as always because although it is now stuffed with advertising hoardings, fundamentally, it does not change. For so many years it has been the main place where we meet our friends, go on dates with our loved ones, see respected elderly people 'aksakals' or 'ustods' and reminisce on the past. Every time I pass near the alley, I always give my word that I will return at the first opportunity.

The city is changing; people are changing, and I feel this especially keenly when I go to the weddings of my friends or relatives. Once, when choosing a bride or groom many questions arose concerning from which region, district, locality, and sometimes even which bystreet the candidate came. Any other nationality was out of the question. Besides this, the genealogy was studied, of what kinship was the person was, their caste, etc. If a guy fell in love, the relatives at home would immediately ask from where his intended came. If a man from the north of the country married a southerner or vice versa - such cases were rare – this was not welcomed by his relatives or friends, and especially his neighbours. Though it may sound ridiculous, it really was that way. Now, everything has changed, and although the question of from where a bride or groom derives from is still asked out of habit, everyone has become accustomed to the fact that young people no longer care about this. As the great Rumi said, it does not matter if you are from the north or the south, the west or the east, the main thing is that you have love for a person in your heart.

I am happy that I have such faithful and sincere friends. They live in many regions, cities and in different countries. I cannot imagine my life without their vibrant participation. Wherever we live, we are united by one main thing - sincere love for our Fatherland, and for its capital, our home-city of Dushanbe.

TRUE PARADISE - LOST PARADISE

The great Jalāl ad-Dīn Rumi said, 'The sweetness and enjoyment of a place of rest are proportional to the troubles of the journey. Only then will you begin to enjoy your hometown and kinsfolk, when you have experienced the tortures of life in exile.'

Have you ever thought that everything in life is repeated? When we are young we are careless and always talking about the future. Then, when we become adults, especially when the first grey hairs appear, as ailments and hard experiences accumulate over the years, we start to look back more, and it seems to us that it was then, in the past, that everything was fine. Nostalgia is a special kind of state, one

which is fundamentally important for comprehending one's life, destiny and position in society. This state comes gradually as if sneaking up, and a person, facing the past, suddenly finds themself in a crowd of acquaintances and strangers who have gathered to mark some sad event. After leaving our Motherland, our home, we often think that everything will be better and start to feel happy. But alas, happiness is not reality, only reminiscences. On relocating to a foreign country not everyone finds understanding and compassion, sometimes even facing hostility and intolerance. Homesickness becomes more and more tangible. Still, culture takes its course, as this is the real need of any given society. Tolerance is a wonderful topic for various kinds of projects and conferences. This is good, but in everyday life we, unfortunately, do not feel it, especially in the CIS countries.

It so happened that during Ramadan I was in London. Before the start of Ramadan, I went shopping to a huge supermarket, Asda (the British arm of the American Walmart Corporation) and saw the following: above each cashier and hanging over every grocery department there was a big poster with an oriental landscape and the words 'Id Mubarak!' I remembered that on the 40th anniversary of the newspaper, *Vechorka*, a video clip featuring 'A Song of Dushanbe' composed by Alexander Zatsepin was shown, which had been professionally made by Iranian cameraman, Mehdi Naini on the orders of the newspaper's chief editor. This clip was uploaded onto YouTube, and was watched by a large audience of about 12,000 people in one day. Many left their comments: 'I had a lump in my throat,' 'It's filmed with love,

thank you!' '*Ich liebe my Heimatsland*, I love you, my native Dushanbe,' 'Thanks to the author. I miss my homeland a lot. I watched and felt heavy in my heart,' 'It's very nice! *Zinda bosh, ey vatan*!' Returning to one's homeland is always pleasant, even if it's through a clip on the internet, you always feel a longing for home, and positive recollections do not leave you.

Having left his homeland, the famous medieval poet, Kamol Khujandi began to write touchingly charming poems about his native land, leaving a whole cycle of ghazals, *Garibi* for us. Having spent half of his life wandering, the great Saadi left wonderful gazelles about his love of his native sources. But, my friends, in order not to be so sick and sad at heart, let us recall careless folklore. They say that time-tested proverbs are irrefragable. For example, 'He who dwells in the past loses sight of the present' (an idiom with the meaning 'let bygones be bygones'). Why so? Maybe, it is a painful condition to feel nostalgia, to feel homesick and to be sad, but perhaps a person cannot live without a sense of bright and aching sadness. As the French poet, philosopher and "apologist" of nostalgia, Marcel Proust stated simply and clearly: 'The only true paradise is paradise lost.'

TIME CONTRASTS

When I walk the streets of my native Dushanbe, I think about the greatness of its most famous representatives of the classical arts. I feel delighted by the uplifting music of the genius Mozart, the creations of Michelangelo or frantic Dali; I recall lines from the poetry of Ferdowsi and Shakespeare or the *Rubáiyát* of jolly Omar Khayyam - his quatrain poetry about life and death, and I try to stay in the moment. In my dreams, they are my supporters, friends and mentors.

A fancy car which drove at speed over loose gravel after a shower brought me back to reality, dousing me with dirty water before rushing away. It was as if it had fulfilled some task. The contrast struck my heart: my dreams and this dirt. How could I avenge that careless driver; shake my fist and follow after him? It would be pointless. Well, God be with him. As Nietzsche said, 'There is as much egoism in generosity as there is in revenge, only this egoism is of a different quality.'

The most crowded crossing in the centre of Dushanbe, the corner of Rudaki Avenue and the House of Press, is known to all the citizens and even to guests in the capital. It is a kind of brand. Here they sell the most marketable food produce in the city, pancakes, and now it is a business, so the product carries a surcharge.

One time when I was buying bread, two untidy boys standing next to me were abusing each other with bold and revoltingly gross expletives. Stopping their talk, I requested that they not bastardise our native tongue. I advised them to read the books of Hafiz, Rudaki, Pushkin and our excellent contemporary writer, Mirzo Tursunzoda. To my query as to whether they knew who Pushkin was, I immediately received the answer: 'Alexander Sergeyevich.' Having not expected such a quick reaction from the boys, who seemed to me to be homeless and hungry, I was agreeably surprised.

I remember well my childhood and youthful impressions from my meetings with the poet, Mirzo Tursunzoda. He and my father walked in the courtyards of our houses in Sviridenko Street (now known as Bukhoro Street). It is as if I hear even now his amazing stories about Tajik-Persian poetry. The timbre of his voice was soft and melodic, especially when he read the Eastern classics.

In the early eighties of the previous century, during the festival 'The Days of Soviet Literature' dedicated to the 70th anniversary of Mirzo Tursunzoda, Honoured Poet of Tajikistan, I was present at the opening of his house-museum. I was entrusted with conducting the first tour with a party of guests comprised of famous figures from the world of literature. Here I met with the outstanding Soviet writer, Chingiz Aitmatov, who told me that he had just been in the birth village of Mirzo Tursunzoda, Karatag. There he had been struck by the fact that young and old alike could recite by

heart verses by Rudaki, Ferdowsi, Khayyam, Hafiz, Saadi, Rumi and Jami, as well as those penned by modern poets.

'Surprisingly, there were grey-haired old men with no education and children of preschool age among them,' Aitmatov said in amazement.

A blank sheet of paper may absorb everything: history, treatise, poetry, prose and notations of our musical heritage. A man, however, that most tragic and happy of creations, cannot in any way assimilate the experience of multiple historical collisions and paradoxical phenomena in the relationship between civilisations. I was fortunate to attend the meetings and discussions of my mentors: Vohid Asrori, Goib Kalandarov and Otakhon Latifi, and to listen to their opinions on numerous philosophical subjects.

In a TV interview in the 1960s, the renowned American writer John Updike called Soviet readers 'amazing people.' He was astounded that people read books whilst sitting on park benches, in elevators and on the subway, and that evening performances by such famous poets as Yevtushenko and Akhmadulina could not accommodate all the spectators hoping to get in.

The world of modern gadgets and Hollywood has imposed the American way of life upon us, but at the same time they have destroyed something which was quivering in our souls. Reflecting on this, philosophers publish treatise referring to the experience of history, believing that culture is just a thin apple peel draped over the red-hot chaos of life. Meanwhile, people on the Earth continue 'to die for metal treasures.'

...Guiltily, those boys at the Dushanbe intersection mouthed the word '*mebahshi*' ('sorry') before more confidently uttering the name of the Russian genius once more, 'Alexander Sergeyevich Pushkin.'

Delivering a speech celebrating the birth of Pushkin, the Russian writer Dostoevsky emphasised in the poet the quality of the 'reincarnation of his spirit in the spirit of foreign nations.' Reading Pushkin's 'Imitations of the Koran,' one cannot fail to feel the high morals of the writer. Goethe's thoughts about Khayyam and Hafiz echo this sentiment. Today, the isolated existence of peoples and cultures is a fiction. That is why the generic consciousness of mankind is returning in a new way, as is the time for the reinterpretation of myths.

'The further we move away from the Soviet era, the more we see that this is not an accidental phenomenon in world history,' Chingiz Aitmatov said in one of his interviews.

Entangled in his arguments about man, God and religion, the German philosopher Nietzsche stated:

To live some right and proper life,
You should be higher than your being.
So, learn to rise above yourself,
To stare down from above at living.

I asked a taxi driver once: 'Why do you speak to me using the pronoun "you" in the singular with so little respect?' He carelessly answered: 'And are you two in number so that

I should address you in the plural?'

That episode brought me to the conclusion that our minds are confused, not because knowledge has turned the world upside down, but because we cannot reconcile with transformational change. We are not psychologically prepared for the secret of the connection between times. Some, in order to comprehend this secret, hasten towards the future, rushing forward, whilst others turn their attention exclusively to the past. Ideas are more conveniently projected when they have been at least partially implemented before. In search of the truth, mankind does not find the proper answers. The Russian poet, Boris Slutsky wrote:

Soon, I'll, or maybe later, disappear to another world,
But unfinished speculation won't stop with my death.
These began long ago, hundreds of years before my birth,
And will last for long, and longer, will continue on this Earth.

...The rain stopped, and it became cool and sunny. I decided not to remember that fancy car which had sped past, splashing mud all over me.

'HOW WONDERFUL IT IS TO LIVE. HOW BADLY WE ARE LIVING...'

The global world begins with a personal one

Once, I arrived in Moscow on a plane crowded with migrant workers, '*Gastarbeiters.*' What a word that is! As I went through customs, I noted how they had stopped a young guy who could not speak a word of Russian. It seemed that his documents were in order, so I became a translator for a while. If I hadn't, my countryman would have had to prove that he was indeed who he said he was for an extended period. The guy was happy with my unexpected assistance, but I became very sad because of him.

Reflecting on the norms of happiness that a person should expect in life, the well-known Russian writer Victor Pelevin argued that no matter what occurs, a certain portion of happiness could not be taken away. One may talk about what is good and bad only when one knows at the very least how and why a person is formed. Do the reasons behind that happiness matter if the happiness produced by different souls is similar?

Sooner or later, everyone searches for the meaning of their existence. Many cannot solve this difficult question. Thank God, there are those who build a temple in their soul. For them, the main thing in life is to understand the following: 'I'll see you off, and I'll be seen off by others.'

Time is the space between an action and its results. Everyone whose life is rich in actions and deeds knows that existence is fleeting. A plane full of young people who, in search of their daily bread, venture into the unknown - this image remains in the memory for a long time. The guy, who spoke an incomprehensible dialect of our native language and could not explain where his surname and his forename were in his passport, had swapped his quiet mountain village for a cruel and unpredictable metropolis in search of happiness. So, by whom and for what was man created? Again, Omar Khayyam's question springs to mind: 'Who are we, and where are we from?'

Sadly, the young man replied to my question, 'where are you going without any professional skills?', that poverty had forced him to travel to distant lands. His father had been killed, and his mother was taking care of ten children. His elder brother had come to Moscow to work two years ago, and they had lost contact with him. 'There is no work there, at home, and even if there is it pays very little,' he said, finishing his unfortunate story. 'All hope for my assistance.'

Later, I had the opportunity to participate at a conference held in London on the development of self-awareness and self-education. Speaking about the true mission of man and mankind, the Head of the Academy, Shaykh Fazlullah said in his report that only a person who knew first-hand what suffering, deprivation and illness felt like could understand another person who was seeking healing and support.

People are united into a single organism which is interconnected by strong ties. Without sympathising with others, first of all, you cannot sympathise with yourself. After all, the global world begins with a personal one. The conference was attended by scientists from different countries who were united by their desire for harmony, compassion and understanding.

The entire cultural and aesthetic heritage of mankind has taught us about beauty and moral virtues. The lessons that books, paintings and musical masterpieces have given us are invaluable. Wisdom should not be complicated, dull or difficult to understand. As relayed in ancient scriptures, the first step towards wisdom is silence, the second is listening, the third is remembering, the fourth is application, and the fifth step is when you can share your accumulated knowledge with others.

How is he now, my fellow traveller, the boy from the distant mountain village? On saying goodbye, I asked him where he was going. 'To Cherkizon,' he answered. 'There are a lot of my native people there, and they will probably help.' Cherkizovsky Market in Moscow is closed now. Where did he go? Maybe he found his brother and settled down somewhere else. God, grant that this is so. Georgy Adamovich was quite right in the verses he dedicated to his fellow Russian poet, Marina Tsvetaeva:

I am not to blame that there is so much pain,
But you, my dear, I am not at all convicting.
All is by chance, all is forced, in vain.
How wonderful it is to live. How badly we are living...

Until a person is capable of mercy, they are not tru-ly alive. A lot of things remain unchanged around us - a lake, a mountain, a river, a spring, a parental home... but something disappears whilst you live. In fact, you lose this 'something' when you irreversibly disregard some important things, and you can only choose the words to describe what is happening in your soul.

A HUMORESQUE

A MEDICAL TREATMENT ROOM

A Story on Behalf of my Friend

Recently the availability of free total prophylactic medical examinations was announced in Moscow and throughout Russia. Elderly people were of concern. It seemed that, after looking at us, the government had decided to extend the retirement age. Note that in the higher echelons of power they do not think about raising pensions and whether they provide enough for the maintenance of health or basic survival needs.

Well, okay, I thought, so upon receiving an invitation I went to a clinic with my wife. We two pensioners were handed a stack of paperwork and asked for samples for laboratory testing.

The next day, early in the morning and on empty stomachs as directed we went to undergo the medical tests, holding each other up by the elbows.

'Galya, you haven't forgotten to bring the requisition order?' I asked upon suddenly remembering.

'No,' Tolenka.'

'And the jars for analysis haven't been mixed up?'

'No, Honey. Although at our age their content doesn't differ much.'

'Well, I am still a male, dear!'

'This question is to be put to me, dear!' my Galya answered with a smile.

So, with this conversation, we reached the clinic. There was a noisy crowd of people outside the treatment room as we joined the queue. Everyone who came carrying jars was being sent to the pharmacy for some reason. I began to listen to the hubbub and realised that Galya and I would have to run there too. It turned out that only samples in special plastic pharmacy containers were being accepted.

The nearest drugstore was closed, so we went to another one.

'Never mind, Galya,' I joked, 'it's good to walk in the morning on an empty stomach. It's as if we're passing an exam for survival.'

'We shall endure everything, of course, but as for the old retired people of the future, it is unlikely,' Galya wheezed, short of breath.

We bought what was required and started back to the clinic. On the way, we met other patients going as fast as they could in the direction of the same chemists. Apparently, like us, they were eager to eat something as soon as possible. As nutritionists recommend, one should eat in small portions but often and, most importantly, at the right times. But how could we have breakfast when everything in our jars had to be moved to other vessels? Sorry for all the unpleasant details!

Finally, we rejoined the queue. People reacted to everything that was happening in various ways, for not only did they have to queue twice, moreover, they had to listen to the comments and reproaches of a nurse.

'Why couldn't they warn us about the pharmaceutical test containers in the first place?' one man grumbled resentfully.

'They could have written an announcement and pinned it on the door!' a second added.

The nurse was both extremely annoyed and afraid that she wouldn't have time to see everyone before a car coming to take the samples to the central laboratory for analysis arrived.

'You are using God knows what for these samples! Aluminium coffee cans, glass jars that have been filled with honey and jam, and it's not even clear what else,' she muttered.

'But it's pretty! Better than in a bottle of milk or beer,' a white-haired fellow wisecracked.

'No!' the nurse barked, shutting him down. 'One patient has just brought his urine in a cognac bottle! Imagine how hard it is for the laboratory assistants. They'll never have time to finish their work.'

One person in the line could stand it no longer and answered:

'They might as well drink it. They say urine is better for you than alcohol.'

Everyone laughed. The nurse's eyes almost popped out of their sockets, but then, seeing the funny side, she laughed too.

Finally, our turn came.

'Where are your requisition slips?' the nurse asked.

We showed her our paperwork.

'You don't need to undergo these tests,' she said, looking upon us calmly, 'only blood tests and fluorography.'

I looked at Galya, and she gazed back at me in amazement and sighed.

'Old age is no fun,' she said. 'And so much running around in vain.'

'Never mind, Galya,' I replied. 'We've certainly worked up an appetite with all that walking. Let's go home and have some breakfast, my dear.'

GALLERY OF PORTRAITS

GENNADY RATUSHENKO
(from an archive)
'A PHOTO IS A VISUAL MEMORY OF HISTORY'

Gennady Ratushenko was born on May the 5th 1941. He graduated from the Omsk Agricultural Institute as an engineer and surveyor. Following his graduation, in 1968 he was sent to Tajikistan, and whilst undertaking aerial photography work he discovered an unexpected passion for photography. For ten years he worked as a photo-journalist for the newspaper *Vecherniy Dushanbe*, and for twenty years he was a special photo-correspondent for the APN and RIA Novosti news agencies. Since 1991, he has been the Chairman of the Union of Photo Artists of Tajikistan. An accomplished author and compiler of six exhibitions and nine photo-albums, for his work he was awarded the Order of Dusti (Friendship).

— *'Gennady Petrovich, your creative work is well-known throughout the Republic. When did it all begin?'*

Frankly speaking, at high school I only received a satisfactory grade in photography. But geodesic practice in the north behind the Arctic Circle and in the Tyumen taiga fascinated me, the pristine beauty forcing me to take up photography seriously. I bought a Zorki-S camera kit, looked through the magazines released by *Soviet Photo* and made friends with Lesha Sushentsov, a cameraman and amateur photographer working on the editorial board of *Omsk TV News*.

I sent photo-stories to the newspapers, *Omskaya Pravda* and *TV News* taken on my student ski trips through the Altai Mountains to Belukha along the alpine paths of the Caucasus. Of course, Lesha Sushentsov helped me select the proper themes from my pile of films. By the way, his TV programs generated from photos were iconic and very clear, beautiful and accurate.

Two years later my passion for photography really yielded fruit when a series of my lyric photos, 'Ascent,' 'Great Sacrament' and 'Love is a Ring' won first prize at the regional photo contest organised by the newspaper, *Omskaya Pravda*.

— 'What do you feel yourself more, a photographer or a photo-artist?'

For me, artistic creativity has always been important. It is banal to talk about a 'third eye,' but I learnt how to see something unusual in ordinary everyday life through the lens. Whilst collaborating with newspapers and television outlets on a freelance basis I received royalties, and photography became my second craft, but my creative one.

— 'I always look through old yellowed photos with pleasure. I think they have more sincerity and purity.'

During the sixties and eighties my passion for photography really blossomed. To me, black-and-white photographs convey the reality of life more reliably, without the distrac-

tion of coloured spots. Colour is the priority for colour photography. In the period of film shortages, black-and-white photography was often used in news stories and industrial programs on TV. Since 1968, I have been collaborating with Dushanbe TV reporters, Mikhail Nikulin and Gennady Shcherbatov and published articles in the Republic newspapers, *Komsomolets Tajikistana*, *Communist Tajikistana*, and my favourite, *Vechorka*.

At the request of Italian artists, in 1980 I prepared an exhibition of one hundred photographs entitled 'Tajikistan and the South of Italy are on One Parallel' and was a participant in the Days of Culture event in this interesting country. The exhibition has been preserved to the present day and would be interesting to a modern audience as well. Today, I still include black-and-white photographs from years past as they beam a positive aura into my colour photographic exhibitions and photo albums.

— 'Life is fleeting, and each of us tries to remember its moments. Often amateur photos are spectacular and emotionally charged, aren't they?'

I agree that today almost every tenth person is an amateur photographer. Many people have mobile phones with a built-in digital camera, a digital snapshot camera and an almost professional camera, and not just the one either. An army of untrained amateur photographers is growing in the capital. After all, there are no professional photographic schools and photo circles here. Not all the faculties of journalism teach photo-journalism even as there still exists a narrow-minded opinion that a camera shoots itself, just click and it's done. Is there anything to study here? The technology of imaging is the same: just project through a lens onto a film or a digital matrix. Digital processing and printing hold more creative opportunities than analogue ones, therefore they have progressed, but for my entire life, I've been learning both from my own mistakes and from the work of my colleagues.

— 'The world is filled with glossy photos. Sometimes smartly published magazines are distributed free of charge. What do you think about the new technology of photo-imaging?'

I look through glossy magazines with a sense of indifference. They are beautiful, catchy, but soulless. I care more about other aspects and outlets. More than eighty galleries opened their doors during the Month of Photography in Vienna, at which I was fortunate enough to participate in November 2006. A hundred of the best photographers were invited to shoot in the Xinjiang Autonomous Region of China in the summer of 2006. There is a House of Photography in Tashkent, and there are numerous photo-galleries in Moscow, but there's no official photo-gallery in Dushanbe. By the way, you don't tend to see these types of glossy photos in photo-galleries expositions. A variety of genres, unusual themes and stories form the basis of exhibitions. Unfortunately, there's nothing to stop and look at in our republican press. Custom, glossy exhibitions, the preparation of which is led by the Ministry of Culture, are not distinguished by

their originality, well-thought-out ideologies or artistic merit. 'I sing what I see,' seems to be the meaning of these exhibitions, but they lack a comprehension of each plot and the image of Tajikistan as a whole.

— 'Each of us has a lot of photo albums and piles of photos from our lives. How should we deal with them? Sometimes it is very difficult to part with memories of the past.'

It is necessary to pity the person who you subject your family photos upon. Select only the important and interesting ones, scan them, copy them to CD-disks and store them for posterity, for their stories. Make digital or analogue photo-albums classified according to topics. The best thing is to entrust your archive to a professional designer who together with your input can help solve this problem. In general, good family photos in beautiful frames of different sizes look great on the walls of an apartment. They create a sense of comfort and carry a positive aura and energy from your ancestors and the time of your youth. Peer at the TV screen; there are many pictures and photos on the walls in any house or office. Do you still have bare walls?

— 'Gennady Petrovich, who do you like to photograph more - children or adults? Or maybe scientists, cultural activists or politicians?'

I'm a professional photographer and should be able to shoot in different genres of photo-journalism and photo-art. Any person remains a person no matter what rank they may hold, and it is always difficult to find their artistic image. I have several photo albums of children of different ages from birth onwards. Twenty years of work as a special photo journalist in Tajikistan at the APN and RIA Novosti news agencies, for magazines and press editions published in foreign countries – this was a great school of journalism!

In terms of the quantity and quality of publications about Tajikistan abroad, I was among the top five photo-correspondents of RVCS (the editorial staff of the All-Union Correspondent Network) and I could have been included into a Tajik Guinness Book of Records if it had existed. Through my photos, people came to understand what kind of country Tajikistan - where 93% of the land is mountainous – is. They learnt about our hospitable people, about the Nowruz holiday and Tajik wedding traditions. I collected a large colour and black-and-white photo library shot during my numerous trips around the Republic in search of interesting images. Unfortunately, as a result of the collapse of USSR, the All-Union Correspondent Network ceased to exist. Many photographers left Tajikistan. I decided to preserve a unique photo library, and not in vain; after all, I photographed and thus helped facilitate the creation of a new history of Tajikistan.

— 'They say that you are the personal photographer of our President?'

President Emomali Rahmon invited me on his trips to the largest construction projects in the Republic and to the opening of new facilities. It was always interesting for me to

shoot images of that big and powerful man in the process of communication with the people and his family. Often, he himself organised scenes and group photos, and we worked as co-authors of a photo. Our picture, 'The President and a Photographer' won the Fuji Film prize at the International Asia-Pacific Photo Contest 'Life in Harmony' in Tokyo in 2000. During the fledgling years of the Republic, I organised an exhibition entitled 'Difficult Roads to Creation' where the main thing was images of the President. I have a lot of thematic photo albums concerning travel reports. He was the designer and compiler of the photo-book, *Tajikistan: 10 Years of Independence*. I compiled and prepared the design of five author's political photo posters and the inauguration calendars of the President for 2007–2008, which were printed in large numbers for the residents of Tajikistan. This is one example of the use of political photography in society. A unique tandem between the President and the photographer was formed, and for me, this was very significant.

— 'What is the guiding principle behind your work, improvisation or a certain scenario according to a production plan?'

Everything flows, everything changes. Sometimes you don't know what will happen tomorrow. If I had had a big legacy, I could have planned unusual subjects, experiments with digital mediums, projects for future photo albums and built or bought a wonderful workshop packed with expensive equipment. In real life, though, it's impossible to plan everything in advance. At some point, you may be deceived, and some people may not fulfil their contractual obligations. I passed through all of those life stages. Most of all, I've been outraged by the lack of commitment of officials who gave their word and then failed to go through with their promises. I adhere to the rule of life: go and work. All the same, sometimes something will work out well impromptu.

— 'Are there any among your published photo albums that you especially cherish? Do you have a favourite snapshot?'

I'd say it's one which wasn't published. The most interesting photo album for me is *Istaravshan is a City on the Silk Road*, which I prepared for the 2,500[th] anniversary of the city which was known as Ura-Tyube in the past. Its interesting history, archaeology, oriental bazaar, craftsmen and cultural monuments enabled me to capture a unique image of this ancient city. One of the famous Moscow photographers once said: 'Well, there is nothing to photograph here!' I had been screening Istaravshan for twenty years. Money was found for the anniversary celebrations, but, alas, it wasn't enough for a print edition. I think it's not too late to publish such a photo album dedicated to the 2,700[th] anniversary of Kulyab: 'The city at the crossroads of epochs' depicted through its history, archaeology and the modern revival of the city and its surroundings.

I would like to make a photo-album called *Ancient Khojent on the Syr-Darya River* about the north of Tajikistan. Sogd, Ashta cave paintings, hiking trails, the pearls of the Fann Mountains, Penjikent, all of this invaluable

photographic material still lies unclaimed beneath a layer of dust. Or an album entitled *Tajikistan: 93% of its Land is Mountains*. The unique photographic material plus the skill needed to compose it correctly would equate to a wonderful work that needs to be published in large numbers. Indeed, there are more than twenty million Tajiks around the globe.

I like my first photo-book, *Tajikistan is the Land at the Feet of the Sun*, and my original photo album with journalistic writings, *Water is Life* is also dear to me. That album was dedicated to the Dushanbe International Freshwater Forum and became a gift for its participants. The album starts with the emblem of the forum and was selected on the basis of its content, which is very significant for a photo-artist. In collaboration with Makhmadsaid Ubaidulloyev, the mayor of the city, I compiled a large anniversary album, *Dushanbe: City of the World* which featured five-hundred photos. That album was published by the professional publishing company, Mega Basim in Turkey.

My favourite snapshot? Photos are my children which I love. There are no unloved children. I am charged with positive energy by my first black-and-white photos, family photos, even amateur ones. A photo is a visual memory of history, and history must be respected for it is our life and our continuation.

— 'I know that your son is also involved in photography. What can you say about his works and will he continue your family's mastery of the art form?'

My son, Julien is a journalism student at RTSU University. Naturally, he is engaged in photography and computer graphics. He feels the colours in a photograph more than me, and all the technical arrangements depend on him. My son is putting my large digital photo library in order.

Creativity is a high bar to which you need to aspire and grow. Julien managed to shoot the smile of the eternally serious RTSU rector and be one of the authors of the photo exhibition, *New Names in Photography*.

— *'Do you have a photo studio?'*

That's a sore subject. In 1996, my colleague bought the two-storey premises of the APS - RIA Novosti news agency at 18 Rudaki Avenue through his own channels. There, on the first floor, was my photo library, the only colour development laboratory in the Republic and Union of Photo Artists of Tajikistan, which we registered with the Ministry of Justice in 1991. I remember the rainy day of Nowruz in 1996, when the new owner suggested dismantling the photo lab and the library and leaving that place which had become so dear to me. I cannot forget that knockout blow and still haven't recovered from it. What's the use of people who privatise for their own profit without giving anything back to the state?

My two-room apartment became the repository of a photo library - the most valuable asset, the history of Tajikistan - and a place for a computer. For the fourth year in a row, the authorities have not given me permission to build an attic over my apartment to use as a workshop. In Astana,

five-storey Khrushchev-era buildings are supplemented with an additional floor on top, a beautiful attic, thus expanding the area for housing. By the way, my original project for a photo gallery, 'Arbat in Dushanbe' in the park named after the 800th anniversary of Moscow was published in *Vechorka* on February 22nd 2007 as a proposal for the improvement of the capital. That project was approved by the mayor of the city and the architects at a meeting of the city council. Instead of a majestic glassy gallery transparent for the inspection of photographs, however, the company, Imperiya Vostok (Empire East) placed a few glazed frames on the wall at Opera and Ballet Theatre as if mocking my project. For whom and for what? So, it remained the lonely, seldom visited cultural centre lost amidst the barbecue smoke, restaurants and pubs. And people want a performance! People want to have a professional studio where they can order a portrait made by a professional photographer, where you can get a wonderful photo for your home, office or summer cottage; a place where it would be possible to get advice on photography and to learn the basics of the art form.

— *'There are a lot of billboards in the city, often tasteless in an aesthetic sense. Have you been approached with proposals to decorate the city with promotional products?'*

Customers wanting promotional materials probably forget that there's a creative Union of Photo Artists which could prepare and fulfil any order for professional advertising with original arrangements. The city is 'decorated' with

billboards featuring strange, non-Tajik photos. Probably, the customers are not patriots.

Life dictates that it's time for creative unions to come together. Therefore, we conducted an experiment. The Union of Photo Artists and the Turkish publishing company, Mega Basim united under one roof in a large building with the Union of Architects. Together, we repaired the interior of the building and, on May 5th 2007, opened a jubilee photo exhibition in honour of my 65th birthday and the 40th anniversary of my photo-journalism work in Tajikistan. It would be logical to find a way to legally secure this House of Architects for our triple alliance, which could become a creative centre for professionals distinguished by their interests. Well, I hope, I hope.

The construction industry is booming in the capital, but expensive walls remain "naked" or decorated with standard posters, low-grade mass-produced images photos or oriental cheap stamped drawings. The architects need to work in concert with photographers, designing in advance a space for photography within offices and for the placement of artistic images on exteriors. Therefore, we're now we creating a large library of interesting images in the hope that they will be in demand.

— 'Let me thank you for a very interesting and informative conversation and wish you, the first photo-journalist of Vecherniy Dushanbe newspaper success and the fulfilment of all your plans.'

MURIVAT BEKNAZAROV

*'I am a Highlander,
and That Says it All.'*
Murivat Beknazarov

AN INTERVIEW WITH MURIVAT BEKNAZAROV, FAMOUS PAINTER AND HONOURED ARTIST OF TAJIKISTAN

— *'Your name, Murivat derives from the word 'muruvvat' and is translated as courageous, noble, courteous, kind and pious. Apparently, your parents put their hearts and souls into it. Please, tell us about your childhood, your family and your first steps as a painter.'*

My parents had four children, and I was the third. When I was three-years-old, we lost my father. Mom had to educate us alone. How much strength and courage it was necessary for her to have in order to feed four small children during those difficult military years! Probably, that's why Mom died so young. We cherish the memory of our mother.

Ever since my childhood, I liked to draw. In those years, children could engage in various extra-curricular activities in schools in addition to their core subjects. I chose the visual arts, and my creative work began with that arts circle.

— *'You grew up in the Pamir mountains. This, of course, could not help but influence you as a painter and muralist. What images, motifs and colours abound in your work?'*

I think that the first impressions of the world surrounding them remain with a person for the rest of their life, and that nature becomes a part of an artist. Over the years these impressions can manifest themselves in unexpected ways, both in terms of perception of the world and in creative activity. For example, when I see some magnificent piece of architecture in Europe or a stunning sculpture in India, I find myself comparing them with the majestic mountains of my childhood. It seems that I became an artist due to an intrinsic need to capture all things mighty and majestic. At the same time, though, for me the more diverse the images and motifs are, the more interesting their embodiment will be, the colour solutions for each painting depending on a specific task.

— *'You work in different genres and are engaged in creating mosaics and murals. Do you place any special emphasis on painting?'*

In Soviet times, much attention was paid to the development of monumental art. I did a lot of work in the fields of mosaic and mural painting in Tajikistan and the other republics. With the collapse of USSR, though, monumental art gradually ceased to exist. And I have always been engaged in easel painting. In painting, I am attracted by the opportunity to rise above the commonplace. I am a highlander, and that says it all.

— 'Your works are exhibited in museums and private collections in France, Italy, Germany, Sweden, Russia, the USA, etc. How often do you exhibit your pieces in Dushanbe?'

Two personal exhibitions have been held in Dushanbe, one in the museum named after Behzod in 1989, and the second in the cultural centre, Bactria in 2002. But let's look back to the past once more. During Soviet times the life of painters was extremely rich; annual republican and all-union exhibitions were held, and the support of the state was felt in everything. A shining example of that was the scholarship of the Union of Artists of the USSR, which was awarded to promising young artists from various republics. Thanks to that scholarship, painters could engage solely in their creative work for two years. At the end of the period, an exhibition of work by the scholars was hosted in Moscow. I was lucky enough to receive such a scholarship in the late 70s, and that served as an incentive for my creative output. Unfortunately, young painters today lack such support.

- 'You studied in Dushanbe, and then in Tallinn. Tell us about your teachers. Among your fellow students are there any whose work you especially value?'

I studied at the Republican Art School from 1958 to1963 in a workshop alongside the talented artists, Besperstov and Safoev. I continued my studies in Tallinn at the Estonian State Art Institute in the Faculty of Monumental Art. I came to the workshop of Professor Valerian Loik, a talented and charming man who'd studied under the supervision of the masters in Paris for twenty years. After graduating from university, I lectured at the Republican Art College named after Olimov in Dushanbe for fifteen years, and then in the Tajik Technical University for nine years. Many of my former students are now successful painters; Azamat Atakhanov (Moscow), Rinat Animaev (Paris), Manuchehr Sabirov (USA), Bahriddin Sanginov (Khojand) and Bakhtiyor Odinaev (Dushanbe) number among them.

— *'What is the source of your inspiration?'*

The source and impulse for inspiration can come from a variety of things: a contemplation of mountain gorges, a conversation with a wise man, a beautiful woman, a fine painting or classical music from any period of time.

— *'What does the common phrase, 'an artist should be free' mean to you?'*

Great artists create things of beauty, because even under conditions where they lack freedom externally, they remain free internally. For an artist, the inner connection with the world and a constant fruitful exchange of energy with nature, people and art is more important than external freedom in all situations.

— *'You served in the ranks of the Soviet Army. What was your rank and do you have any interesting recollections from your time spent in military service? What would you wish to say to today's soldiers and military men?'*

I was enlisted to serve in Tashkent as a graphic designer

to a military unit. The commander and the deputy political officer of our unit made a big impression on me; I seldom met such clever and erudite military men. And what a library we had! Our unit was the most professionally and colourfully decorated in the whole division owing to my efforts. I would like to wish a good education and love for their homeland to today's soldiers and servicemen; may they serve their country faithfully.

— *'Tell us about an unforgettable event in your life.'*
My trip to India and Nepal in 1990, during which I came into contact with the ancient culture of those fabulous countries. A thousand-year-old sculpture and certain wall paintings made a special impression on me. I love ancient art, the great creations of Greek and Roman sculptors and architects, but what I saw in India and Nepal was beyond words.

— *'You are an artist, and your spouse, Lola Tolis is a composer. They say that two creative people rarely get along in one house. Is this really true?'*
On the key thing, we have a common understanding: our attitude towards life and art, and our interest in each other's work. Any remaining differences are trifles which are easily surmountable.

I will conclude my conversation with Murivat Beknazarov with the words of the German conductor, Pierre-Dominique Ponnelle:

'I have travelled around the world a lot and met many artists, but the genuine ones are few and far between. Murivat Beknazarov is one.'

A PRELUDE TO NOWRUZ

ZARRINA MIRSHAKAR

There are people with whom you always feel comfortable. It's easy to communicate with them because their soul is in full view. For more than forty years I have been closely acquainted with Zarrina Mirshakar, a beautiful person and a talented composer. Every meeting with her is cordial, sincere, and brings forth unique moments.

Nowruz is a double holiday for Zarrina: both New Year according to the Eastern calendar as well as her birthday. It was on Nowruz that she kindly agreed to answer my questions.

— 'They say that talent is the synthesis of inspiration gifted from above and of experience gained on the Earth. Creatively gifted people prove the divine principle through their works. How do you think this happens?'

In my opinion, talent is an innate quality, and that says it all. It either exists, or it does not. When we see stunning children's drawings or hear a child playing a musical instrument magnificently, we say 'How gifted he is!' We don't speak about skill and experience acquired and stored over the years. According to the composer, Pyotr Tchaikovsky, inspiration is a guest who does not like to visit lazy people.

You must work every day, believe, be in constant search of inspiration and it will come to you. Therefore, I think, talent is a synthesis of inspiration, experience and great diligence; this is what leads to the emergence of outstanding creations.

— 'You come from the very famous family of Mirsaid Mirshakar, a National Poet of Tajikistan. Is talent inherited? By the way, this is a poem that the pianist, Sergey Arzumanov sent to you from New York:

> Everyone knows, old and young,
> That Zarrina Mirshakar
> In her 'Bytes' piano plays,
> Tells the children national tales,
> Having inherited from her father,
> Mirsaid, the learned Elder,
> The gift to touch a lyric string
> That love for the native land will bring.

How nice and unexpected; my thanks to Sergey for remembering me!

I'm happy that I was born into such a creative family. Papa Mirsaid Mirshakar was not just a well-known poet; he also drew beautifully and loved music. My mother, Gulchehra always inspired us with her optimism. She loved to sing and dance since her voice was naturally beautiful. She also knitted excellently.

Talent is a gift from God and it must be nourished at home and at school and be guided in the right direction. We

children were very lucky that our family always had such a creative atmosphere. Our parents often took us to the theatre. In the evenings, poets and composers gathered in our house, reading their new verses and playing their new works on the piano. No matter where we went with our parents in the summer, we always visited concert halls, theatres and museums. My brother, Akmal is now a recognised artist and his paintings adorn private collections around the world. All four of his children draw wonderfully, and his daughter, Rukhmina writes poetry. My sister, Zulfiya also writes beautiful poems and stories, and my brother, Afzal is a master of couplets and an excellent storyteller.

— 'After graduating from the Dushanbe Music School, you continued your education in Moscow with outstanding teachers in the best conservatory in the world. What memories from this time do you hold especially dear?'

My first meetings with the composers, Yuri Ter-Osipov, Sergey Balasanyan and Eduard Hagagortyan. Subsequently, they became my teachers with whom I stayed in touch until the last days of their life.

My father was a member of the Lenin and State Prizes Committees. On one occasion he took me to a meeting - I will never forget that day. There, I met with Dmitri Shostakovich, Aram Khachaturian and Nikolai Tikhonov. Taking advantage of the moment, I showed my preludes to Dmitri Dmitriyevich (Shostakovich) and was surprised by his quiet, even a little shy mannerisms. Both timidly and delicately, he impressed upon me that one had to work hard. I am sorry that I never took photographs; imagine what an archive I would have! Travels, meetings with fellow musicians from near and far - all of these things have been unforgettable. My friends, Guldjamilya from Almaty, Katya Konovalenko from Germany, Dushan Mikhalek and Benjamin Yusupov from Israel, and Radan Vranesevich from Italy have always supported and continue to support me. To paraphrase Hemingway, I want to say that whatever I do for the rest of my life, these moments will stay with me.

— *'**Here's another surprise; kind words from your friends in Israel and closer to home.**'*

Benjamin Yusupov, composer and conductor:
'I consider Zarrina Mirshakar to be one of the most talented Tajik composers. Her creativity is the clearest example of combining deep folk principles with a great degree of skill and elegance in her compositions. She is a highly educated person and has always been an example for me of a true Tajik lady.'

Dusan Mikhalek, musicologist:
'Your *Bytes* was played by Daniel Detoni, a young pianist from Croatia, the son of the composer, Dubravka, and was hugely appreciated by the audience. I announced to the public that you had dedicated those pieces of music to me. So, your music was played in the holy city of Jerusalem.'

Larisa Nazarova, musicologist, PhD in art history, associate professor at the Tajik National Conservatory:

'Though works by Zarrina may be relatively small in number, each piece is imbued with a great deal of creativity. Proof of this can be seen by the fact that her *'A Poem-Sonata for Clarinet Solo'* was included in the compulsory program of the competition for clarinettists in Leningrad in the 1980s. The style of this composer, unlike of all the others, is expressed by the dialect of Pamir speech. Pamir folklore and associated artistic values are the basis of her music, and are realised at the level of language, drama and ideological concept. The category of the national is changeable in the works of Zarrina Mirshakar, but carries on traditions through a process of renewal. I will list the composer's works: a symphony, a symphonietta, a symphonic poem *'Colours of the Solar Pamir,' 'Pamir Pictures,' 'A Poem-Sonata for Clarinet Solo,' 'A Sonata for Oboe Solo,' '24 Bytes'* – a piece of music for a piano, and a concertino, *'Respiro for a Violin, a Chamber Orchestra and Timpani.'*

— *'**Which of your creations is your favourite?**'*
I love all of the works. They are all different, but I left a piece of my soul in each. Of course, it's nice to hear glowing words from such experts.

— *'**What do you think modern music is? In our time, we hear a lot of controversial judgments, as, indeed was the case in the era of our fathers'.**'*
Back in the day, one of the poets said that high mod-

ern technology has taken composers too far and their works were becoming something beyond the level of human perception. The new in music, poetry and painting is not always accepted, and certainly not by everybody at once. Understanding comes gradually. It takes time to comprehend, to filter through oneself, adopt innovative forms and ideas and choose whether or not to use them in one's work. At one time, *A Village Symphony* by Mozart wasn't approved of by the public, though that work was later recognised as a masterpiece. The impressionists, modernists and avant-gardists all passed along a difficult path on their way to recognition. The emergence of the New-Vienne school of Schoenberg, Webern, Berg was received ambiguously, but time has shown that their creations were a new page in the music of the twentieth century.

Nowadays, modern composers use electronic and computer equipment. But we have had no opportunity to hear these kinds of work on the stage, so I cannot say whether I like them or not.

— *'They say that our national conservatoire in the Republic opened too late, but better late than never. Is it possible to solve the problems of the development of modern musical art only with the help of such an institution?'*

The opening of the conservatoire is a gift from President Emomali Rahmon for us, workers of art. Taking advantage of the moment, I would like, on my own behalf and on behalf of the whole team, to express our gratitude to the President.

The Conservatoire is young and, of course, we have problems, such as a lack of professional staff and educational published materials. Unfortunately, there are only a few students in the faculties of string and brass. This may lead to a situation in the future where there will be nobody to employ in the orchestra for the opera theatre, for example. I think this is due to the fact that after graduating from the Republican Secondary Special Music School named after (n.a.) Shahidi, a school n.a. Malika Sobirova, and a college n.a. Bobokulova, students go to other universities and not to the conservatoire. Another problem is the location of special music schools. Recently, teachers at the conservatoire and cultural figures signed a letter to the President asking that the Republican Secondary Special Music School be relocated to the city centre. Now, thank God, this has been set in motion. We really hope there is a building (closer to the conservatoire), and the school will be replenished with gifted children who want to study music. Hopefully, in ten years - the results would not take long - there will be a new desire and aspiration.

— '*At the concert dedicated to the anniversary of Shostakovich, a new vocal cycle written by you was performed. I communicated with musicians who spoke very warmly about your creative work. I would like to give you some feedback.*'

Nighina Obidova, Associate Professor at the Tajik National Conservatory:

'Zarrina and I have known each other for many years.

First of all, I want to say that she is a wonderful person and a great composer. Her compositions for piano and chamber ensembles are a brilliant synthesis of the aesthetics of Pamir melodies and the attitudes of their author. The composer dedicated the piece for piano, 'Bliki' (2003) to me, and I became the first to perform it. It is with great pleasure that I play her pieces for piano and violin ensembles. 'Three Pamir Murals' for violin and piano was performed just the other day in Paris by our violinist, Shafak Kasymova to rapturous applause.'

Oyat Sabzalieva, People's Artist of Tajikistan, Professor at the Tajik National Conservatory:

'One could speak about Zarrina for hours and say only good things. We lived in the same room in the hostel of the Moscow State Conservatory. I remember that at six o'clock in the morning when the Soviet anthem sounded over the radio, she was already in a tutorial room preparing for classes. It was with particular excitement and diligence that she prepared for a class taught by Sergey Balasanyan. He literally devastated her with his exacting requirements. He was particularly strict and uncompromising.

'Once, I had a great evening where I sang in the small hall of the conservatoire. There were many friends and acquaintances there which, of course, included Zarrina. Afterwards, upon my return to the hostel, I saw a beautifully laid table. This was the work of my best friend, Zarrina. Today, I want to wish her good health and considerable success in her creative endeavours.'

On Wikipedia, it is written about my companion and friend Zarrina Mirshakar that she is the 'first and the only female composer of the Pamir… the first female composer in Tajikistan.' I would like to add that the name 'Zarrina' means light, strong, golden, radiant and shining like the sun at dawn. Long may you continue to shine and make us happy, Zarrina!

A WOMAN
OF STRONG CHARACTER
GULCHEHRA SHARIPOVA

Gulchehra Sharipova, PhD in Political Science and First State Counsellor of Justice is one of those women who upon meeting you will remember for the rest of your life. Educated, erudite and successful at work, she is always friendly and interesting to talk to. In addition to the above and her role as a wife and a tender mother, Gulchehra also writes poetry.

— 'Gulchehra, what do you think about the International Women's Day holiday?'

I'm surprised that it only lasts for one day. Our women earned the right to attention and equality long ago. They suffered through all the burdens of hard times alongside men. By the way, have you ever asked yourself why there is not a single monument dedicated to a woman in our beloved Dushanbe? Aren't there any worthy ones? What about Zebunniso, the great poet? Or Zainabbibi, a heroine in the formation of Soviet power in Tajikistan? Or Malika Sobirova, the glorious and world-famous ballerina? At the very least there should be a monument to mothers.

— 'Indeed, there is no such monument. I hadn't even considered it. How do you evaluate the role of a businesswoman in modern Tajikistan?'

Oh, I have very high requirements for such women. A businesswoman, in my opinion, is above all else an official. First, she must be competent in her work and correct in her communication. She should not know any conceit or arrogance. It is always ridiculous to look at people - not just women - who engage in egoism, proudly looking down at everyone from the lofty heights of their self-importance, which is most often illusory. Of course, you can be proud, but only of real achievements, not of a temporary occupation or of some position. A businesswoman should be distinguished by the ability to dress in a not overtly modern fashion, but stylishly. The most essential component of her personality, however, is her intelligence.

— 'Is it easy for a woman to fit in the sphere of a public office?'

It's not easy, but it's necessary. Honestly, as a woman, people tend to judge you too much based on your appearance.

— 'Can a woman keep up everywhere: at work, at home, and still look well?'

Maybe, if she really wants it. Everything is in her hands.

— 'Do you have time for everything?'

I sometimes work 24-hours a day.

— 'And what about your family?'

My family is everything to me. I'm convinced that all successes in your career depend on the atmosphere in your family.

— *'What are the main fields of your activity?'*

The problems of international relations, registration of regulatory legal acts of ministries and departments, the institute of advanced training of justice personnel and others.

— *'You are known as a woman of strong character. Who influenced the formation of your character?'*

My father, Holbobo Sharipov, who trained many famous athletes, had a tremendous impact on me. Dad was a bright, noble and strong man, extremely simple and very easy to talk to. His main motto was modesty. For him, everyone was equal, from a high official to a simple farmer. He didn't let stardom go to his head. He was cheerful and good-natured but at the same time a plain-spoken and intransigent person able to express his opinions fearlessly and honestly regardless of the consequences. He couldn't bear intrigue, falsehood and sycophancy. Dad was always ready to support anyone who needed his help, and people loved him for it.

— *'You possess the qualities of a leader; did your father contribute to this?'*

Of course. First of all, he placed his deep trust in me. He never fell foul to petty suspicion, was extremely open with me and saw and respected me as a person. Only once in his life, I was a schoolgirl at the time, did he say to me: 'Daughter, do not let me down!' These words stuck fast in my mind. Dad has not been with us for a long time, but I still try not to let him down.

— *'A woman in a position of responsibility, will this become a more regular occurrence, or is it an anomaly?'*

Nowadays, it's quite common. The famous Decree of the President of the Republic of Tajikistan 'On enhancing the role of women in society' of 1999 has had its effect. Now, a woman in public office is not a wonder.

— *'It seems to me that a female politician is a very rare phenomenon in our modern society. Can a woman ever become the President of Tajikistan?'*

Why not? Our glorious Tajik land has given birth to many talented sons and daughters. Maybe, a young girl is already growing up somewhere who will lead our country one day. As you know, the East has always been famous for the wisdom of its women. After all, it is no wonder that it is in the East that women have most often occupied the post of head of state or government. Recollect, for example, Indira Gandhi in India, Sirimavo Bandaranaike in Sri Lanka, Corazon Aquino in the Philippines, Benazir Bhutto in Pakistan, and Tansu Çiller in Turkey. They were in no way inferior to men in terms of their leadership.

— *'For some reason, though, our mentality, especially in rural areas, does not allow a woman to put herself above a man in solving many everyday issues. Do women know their rights?'*

Rights are rights, but this knowledge should not be used as a means for confrontation in family relationships. It is necessary for an intelligent woman not to put herself above her husband, even if in some way he is inferior to her. The strength of a woman is to be able to keep the peace in the household alongside that knowledge.

— *'Would you like to live in an epoch of matriarchy?'*
No.

— *'Are there limits to what is acceptable for men and for women'?*
I would say this: what is permissible for men is often unforgivable for women.

— *'Does the harmony of family relations and the warmth of a family hearth depend only on a woman?'*
The "weather" in a house depends on the wife. This is my firm conviction. In the home, a hurricane, complete calm or a light breeze under the soft sun are all the handi-work of the wife.

— *'Tell me, are there any character features you dislike in yourself?'*
Outspokenness; but I cannot behave otherwise, or it would be insincere. Yes, even credulity, perhaps.

— *'Have you been deceived often?'*
Infrequently; but if this happens then I lose faith in a person forever.

— *'Due to the nature of your service, you work most often with men. Do you feel they indulge or condescend to you?'*

There is no unambiguous answer. In my understanding, service is an open, honest and equal partnership. If this is not the case, then the work becomes uninteresting.

— *'What can unpleasantly surprise you in some men?'*

The presence of female traits in their character.

— *'Namely?'*

Their inclination to gossip.

— *'I've noticed that you like to answer briefly, so I'll ask blitz questions. How would you characterise a foe?'*

As a driving force, owing to which you progress.

— *'And stinginess'?*

An eternal swamp. No matter what falls there, everything is sucked down, and it's still not enough.

— *'Jealousy'?*

This is probably the envy of a covetous person.

— *'Stupidity?'*

Boundless emptiness.

— 'Sometimes, we women can feel melancholy. What do you do when you feel restless?'

In moments of sadness, I listen to classical music, especially the works of Aram Khachaturian and Ravel. I also love Verdi.

— 'And of the modern singers, who do you like?'

I love songs performed by Zemfira and Daler Nazarov.

— 'What would you like to say to the female half of the world on this festive day?'

I wish all women to feel, care, pay careful attention to and show deep respect and sincere love to their menfolk, not only on this one day but throughout the whole year. And for those who have no family yet, I wish for them to gain confidence and have a happy future. Towards this, we should all strive with an open heart and heavenly thoughts.

TRAVEL SKETCHES

SO NEAR AND SO FAR AWAY, AMERICA

In life, I am a sentimentalist, and I like to travel. I remember the words of my grandmother when I was a child: '*Didagiatu hondagiat memonad,*' which translates from Tajik as 'Only the things that we have seen and read remain.' She taught us, her grandchildren, not to engage in the accumulation of material goods, but rather to spend money to see the world and read more. I understand her better now than I did as a child. She was descended from the famous and rich tribe of servants of the Emirate of noble Bukhara. Bibidzhon (grandmother) was an educated woman, a rarity for that time. With the arrival of the October Revolution from Russia, her family lost everything in

a day. My grandmother had to work as a teacher in a rural school whilst raising five children alone. A well-known orientalist, her husband, my grandfather was first imprisoned for his genealogy and then sent to the front, dying bravely whilst fighting the fascists. All of their children obtained a higher education. Grandma loved to repeat that everything in life is perishable. Only memory is immortal.

So, it turned out that I inherited from my bibidzhon a love of books and travelling. Later, to my surprise, I became a writer myself. I am grateful that my compatriots in the many corners of the Earth invite me to presentations and creative evenings. I am happy to travel and meet my readers thanks to my three sons, who always support me in this. Not long ago, I was invited to New York and Washington. Honestly, I doubted whether I could endure the long flight given my advancing years

My friends organised the trip, namely Irena Arzutova, a promoter, producer and director of ARZ-Opera Production Centre and David Gvinianidze, President and Artistic Director of the Talents of the World Foundation. In New York, I was met by friends and relatives: Husravbek Murodov, my nephew Parviz Shahidi, a son of friends of our family, and Natalia Kordo, the main organiser of the evening, a program manager at Devidzon Radio, broadcasting in the city in English and Russian. The majority of the audience hailed from the former Soviet Union, including, of course, the republics of my native Central Asia. In advance of my arrival, Natalya Kordo had conducted an interview with me which had been transmitted and repeat-

ed on Devidzon Radio for the whole week together with advertising about the upcoming event.

On the night, representatives of many nationalities who spoke Russian gathered in a small and cosy concert hall at the radio centre. My nephews, Parviz and Joniz, who'd recently settled in Brooklyn, helped me to host the occasion. The audience listened with interest to the story of the genesis and release of my books, *My Neighbourhood Sisters* (stories about the fates of Tajik women) and the academic book about the genius of translation, V. A. Zhukovsky, *I am Looking Towards the East*. There were a lot of questions and feedback.

Here, to my joy, I met Tochiniso Raupova, a friend with whom I'd worked for many years at the Academy of Sciences of Tajikistan. She'd come especially from Maryland to see me. When Tochiniso spoke, one of those present asked me: 'Is this your editor, Vera?' (which translates as 'Faith'). 'Yes, I am faith and hope and love,' Tochiniso replied, 'but my surname is not Deinichenko.'

Shortly, I became acquainted with another Tochiniso, a relative of my friend. So, I walked between the two Tochiniso throughout my stay in New York, making many wishes according to ancient superstitious beliefs. I sincerely thank them for their attention, support, and for showing me the many sights of the city. I also managed to meet with my relative, Rasuli from Samarkand, and Zarnigor and Nozijon, the cute daughters of my friends.

The hotel where I was staying, the Pierre was part of the chain of Indian Taj hotels, most likely named after the Taj Mahal Palace. It was located in Manhattan, near Central Park. Due to the time difference, I woke early the next morning. It was very warm, so I opened the window. Imagine my surprise when I heard Tajik speech on the streets. I learnt that young Tajik guys from Samarkand were working as cab drivers on beautifully decorated phaetons in the park from early in the morning so as to be the first in line. Their names were Bekhruz, Iskandar and Chamshed. They took kids for rides through the huge park and earned their living by doing so.

The second day turned out to be even more intense. The Chairman of the Central Asian Public Foundation in New York, Ashraf Zakirov called me to request an interview. He told me that the Foundation published the magazine, *The Voice of the East* in Russian, Tajik and Uzbek, and provided content for radio and television broadcasts. Despite the distance from Manhattan to Brooklyn, I didn't feel tired and was pleased to meet Shavkat Ashti, a well-renowned figure and now a *Voice of the East* radio presenter. A Tajik singer and event announcer, he has been living in New York for many years. That was his first online radio interview for the Central Asian Foundation which began broadcasting on that very day. So, I became the first guest to enter the studio.

I could speak about the numerous sightseeing tours and trips around the city for a long stretch of time. One cannot get around New York in the space of five days, but I managed to visit the main attractions. According to guidebooks, New York includes five areas situated where the Hudson River meets the Atlantic Ocean. In the centre of the city, densely populated Manhattan is one of the world's largest commercial, financial and cultural centres. There are numerous skyscrapers, including the Empire State Building, and the huge Central Park. The Broadway Theatre is located at Times Square illuminated in neon lights. Dedicated to September 11, the Memorial Complex was built in commemoration of the victims of the terrorist act that occurred on that spot in 2001. This location is also known as Ground Zero. The terrorist act of September 11 took the lives of 2,977 people, thus becoming the largest terrorist attack in world history in terms of the number of victims. Of course, I also visited the Statue of Liberty, the Metropolitan Museum of Art, Carnegie Hall, the famous Brooklyn Bridge, the Bull in Wall Street, the Hudson River and the beautiful shore of Atlantic Ocean.

On the fifth day, I took a train to Washington on the invitation of Farhod Salim, Ambassador of the Republic of Tajikistan to the United States of America. My friends were already waiting for me at the train station, my colleague the journalist Umed Babakhanov and his wife among them. An intellectual and spiritual person, Umed is a well-known media magnate in Tajikistan. I am ashamed to confess it, but in Dushanbe we've never had a chance to communicate as much as we did during those days in Washington. I met Umed's beautiful family, his sons, daughter-in-law, relatives and friends. They graced my stay in Washington and took care of me, especially Umed's wife, dear Firuza, who constantly called, invited

and showed me the sights of the capital. She repeatedly said that my visit was too short and time should be used efficiently.

A presentation of the books, *My Neighbourhood Sisters*, *Farhod from Navgilem*, *I am Looking Towards the East* and a meeting with compatriots was hosted in our embassy. I was glad that such good diplomatic personnel had been raised in the Republic. Farhod Salim is a very erudite and competent young diplomat. Seeing such young, responsible and promising personnel, we can confidently say that Tajikistan has a great future. A publication by the Eurasian Creative Guild devoted to North America, *OCA Magazine* was also presented at the meeting. The participants were interested in an article about the Embassy of the Republic of Tajikistan in the United States and the activities of its ambassador, Farhod Salim.

The meeting with my readers was very warm and relaxed. I was pleased that my books had touched the hearts of people. I especially remember the conversations with my fellow countrywomen, Farida Asadova and Shahnoza Yakubova, who have been living far away from their homeland for so many years. At the meeting, I became friends with Marina Abrams, a member of the European Creative Guild and the author of a wonderful children's book, *Blue Domes and Orange Roofs*, which she presented. She told me that the book was being prepared for a print-run in an English-language edition. Before the meeting concluded, there were many questions about life, family and creativity. I tried to answer everyone because I

felt how sincerely happy my family and friends were with my success.

Whilst in Washington I made friends with two more ladies, Dili (Dilorom Baratova) and Dila (Dilafruz Juraeva). Again, I was able to make wishes between two people with similar names. Together, we looked at the famous buildings where the three branches of US power are situated: the Capitol, the White House and the Supreme Court, before visiting a museum and the concert hall of Kennedy Centre.

In the words of the Russian singer and poet, Vyacheslav Butusov, 'Goodbye, America!' I really hope to return someday, as I have left a piece of my heart with my friends there.

REFLECTIONS AT THE TEMPLE
OF THE HOLY SEPULCHRE

They say everything is in the hands of God,
and life confirms it.

I was incredibly lucky: I had received an invitation from Israel to present my books in Tel Aviv. Entitled 'And a Soul Speaks to a Soul,' my creative evening was organised by Irena Arzutova, the President of the ARZ-Opera Production Centre, with the support of the Russian Cultural Centre. My young friend Irena is a member of the Eurasian Creative Guild. She did everything together with her spouse to make my stay in Israel memorable.

The presentation of my books published in Moscow and London was held in a convivial atmosphere. Those present asked me a lot of questions about Tajikistan and its wonderful people, and about the difficult period following the collapse of USSR, which saw civil war break out in the Republic in the 1990s. I told them about the nonfictional heroes of my books, *The City Where Dreams Come True*, *My Neighbourhood Sisters* and *Share Love*, and saw genuine interest and empathy in the eyes of the audience. My academic works, *A Sentimental Journey or All in Good Time*, a study of the literary ties between Russia and Tajikistan in the 1920s and 1930s, and *I am Looking Towards the East*, a book about the translations of V.A. Zhukovsky were not left unattended. A clip about Dushanbe and an excerpt from T. Shahidi's film, *Khayyam's Rubais* featuring the great ballerina Malika Sobirova was also shown before Irina Bertman, a prima singer of the Tel Aviv Opera Theatre performed a vocal cycle composed by Tolib Shahidi, the famous Tajik composer.

During my visit, I was particularly struck by a trip to the holy city of Jerusalem, the cradle of mainstream religion in the world. I am a Muslim, Irena a Hebrewess and Svetlana a Christian, but in that place, we all became as one, just like the numerous pilgrims who had flocked to the Holy Land on that day. We also visited the Alexander Nevsky Monastery, the Wailing Wall, the White Mosque and the Church of the Holy Sepulchre. I can hardly describe my impressions in their entirety, but the thought it brought into focus in my mind was that God is one, Almighty and Human-Loving. He does not divide people into representatives of different

religions and denominations. God is merciful and forgives everything.

At the Wailing Wall, people quietly sobbed and prayers were said. When I laid my head against the wall, I felt as if my mother had stroked my forehead with her hand. In Lavra earlier, I had recalled to Irena that my mother, a blue-eyed, pale-skinned woman, was known as 'Aunt Masha' in Dushanbe, and my mom had heard me and accepted my pilgrimage. Remember, once upon a time Muslims began their hajj from Jerusalem, back when it was still known as Bait-ul-Muqaddas.

We spent a long time at the Wailing Wall. The day was very hot and there were many pilgrims. When we climbed back up the steep steps, we didn't feel any fatigue. As if some wings were carrying us, there was no heaviness or shortness of breath, but comfort in our hearts and spiritual peace. Such a pilgrimage was like sanctification: you forget about offences; you forgive everyone and beg for forgiveness from God.

ITALY: THE BAY OF POETS
AND A NEW CENTRE OF HIGH ARTS

The Bay of Poets is a beautiful inlet on the east coast of Liguria in the town of Lerici. It is one of the most famous places in Italy. In the first half of the 19th century, these lands were not yet known outside of Italy. The beauty of the Ligurian coast was appreciated by foreign visitors for the first time by British people of arts. In the 1820s, English poets George Gordon Byron and Percy Bysshe Shelley settled there.

It is in this beautiful city at the Bay of Poets that an annual festival of classical music, choral singing and musical and poetic art is held. As if by some mystical coincidence or divine plan, we participants of the festival were staying in the villa where Percy Bysshe Shelley, the famous English

romantic poet lived and often met his with his friend, the renowned poet, George Byron. To quote from the Russian poet, Alexander Blok's *Poets lived here*: 'They lived in Lerici on the east side of the bay. Shelley had a wife Mary, who was the author of the famous novel *Frankenstein*, and Byron lived with his girlfriend Claire Clairmont.' The following verses by Shelley spring to mind:

> When the lamp is shattered
> The light in the dust lies dead—
> When the cloud is scattered
> The rainbow's glory is shed.
> When the lute is broken,
> Sweet tones are remembered not;
> When the lips have spoken,
> Loved accents are soon forgotten.

Starting on the 15th of August, for two weeks concerts were performed every evening in the Bay of Poets. The main venue was the Old St. Francesco Church, where the opening and closing of the festival and large concerts were held. I was impressed by the sincere involvement of the head of the city, departmental officials and church ministers.

On the third day of the festival, works by my husband, Tolib-khon Shahidi were performed. The entire concert was dedicated to the great teacher and world-famous composer, Aram Khachaturian, and to his student and successor, Tolib Shahidi. I was astonished that all the places were occupied, and many people who had no place to sit stood for the duration of the concert listening to the music. It was unforgettable.

The world premiere of *A Concerto for a Viola and a Symphony Orchestra* composed by Tolib Shahidi was performed. Maxim Novikov, a virtuoso violist played the solo part, and Gianluca Marciano, the General Director of the festival conducted. Fragments from Tolib Shahidi's ballet, *The Death of an Usurer* were also performed. The second part of the concert was dedicated to musical masterpieces by Aram Khachaturian.

Following the concert, we decided to travel around Italy for a while. We went to Pisa to see the famous tower. Pisa is a city of Greek origin, a fact which determined the configuration of churches and castles buildings. Numerous magnificent towers, historic buildings and beautiful residences seem to be "hiding" in this city. Florence is located nearby, so how could we miss visiting that city founded in the 1st century BC? It is full of majestic cathedrals, chic villas and palazzo, verdant gardens and other amazing places. It left unforgettable impressions which there are barely words to describe.

The Cathedral Square is located in the historic centre of the city in which the Cathedral of Florence solemnly stands, surrounded by a bell tower and a baptistery. This place has been causing exclamations of admiration and the purest of spiritual impulses among tourists for a long time. It is worth plotting the route of your walk around Florence from here.

Ponte Vecchio, or the Old Bridge is the most venerable crossing over the Arno River, and, at the same time, its

main decoration. Originally constructed in the 10th century, the current structure dates to the 14th century and has been preserved in a practically unchanged form to the present day. The bridge is especially original as houses are located on both sides directly above the water.

The church of San Lorenzo is the most famous Florentine tourist attraction. This Christian church dating from the 4th century was renovated in a Romanesque style in the 11th century. In the Middle Ages, the founding father of Renaissance architecture, Brunelleschi reconstructed it significantly, and the Medici family took charge of the temple. Its basilica has impressive interior decoration which includes a white and gold ceiling, a decorated dome and works by the finest architects of the epoch. The temple is best known, however, as the burial site of the Medici princes.

The Uffizi Gallery is located a ten-minute walk from Piazza della Signoria and is not difficult to find if one strolls towards the Arno River. This medieval palace is filled with the most valuable canvases by Italian, Flemish and other European artists. Owing to their connections and wealth, the founders of the gallery, the Medici acquired real masterpieces. To see all the sights, we would have had to stay for at least ten days, but as that was not possible we just got wants and needs met.

To be the spouse of a creative person is not at all easy. I first heard those words from Markhabohon, my mother-in-law and the wife of the famous Tajik composer, Ziyadullo Shahidi. I was reminded of them once again by Aram Khachaturian, my husband's teacher at the conservatory on the

day of our first meeting. 'Gulya, my dear flower,' he told me, 'you do not even understand what a rope you are placing around your neck. To be the wife of a real composer is not an easy job, and Tolib is an inexhaustible fountain of creativity.' Now I have become a writer, I know just how important the support of loved ones is.

There are moments in life when you forget all the difficulties and become excited all over again by written works. I was lucky twice: I not only saw what was written by my husband, but also heard his music in the best concert halls in the world.

A NEW MEETING
IN ZHUKOVSKY'S HOMELAND

Thirty-five years ago, I travelled to the Tula Region of Russia on a business trip. At that time, I was working at the Institute of Language and Literature named after Rudaki as part of the Academy of Sciences of Tajikistan, and was researching the theme, Zhukovsky and the East. I'd been to the libraries of Moscow and Leningrad to rummage through the archives, where I found valuable facts about the poet's biography and creative activity. There were a few documents concerning my chosen topic in Tula Region, though, the birthplace of Vasily Andreyevich Zhukovsky, a teacher of the crown princes and the great Pushkin. I wrote a research paper on the translation activities of Zhukovsky related to the theme of the East, but it was not possible to publish it. It laid on my table for exactly for thirty years.

All in good time, though. In 2015, I published my first book, *The City Where Dreams Come True*. Having learnt about my research on Zhukovsky, my friend and editor Vera Deinichenko insisted on its publication. She was interested to learn more about her "countryman." After all, she lived and worked in the city of Suvorov in the Tula Region, close to Belyov, the birthplace of the Russian poet and the translator. There were lingering doubts in my mind, but you do not know my friend. She categorically insisted upon the publication of the academic study, *I am Looking Towards the East*, on which we worked with great interest and excitement.

After the book was published, Vera organised a presentation in the district library of Suvorov City, an invitation which I gratefully accepted. A whole band gathered together, my friends, former Dushanbe residents Lyudmila Sinitsyna and Nazokat Kholova, my neighbour and her daughter, Tanya. We travelled by car with Farrukh, my countryman from Khojand who immediately became acquainted with everyone. Arriving in Suvorov, we were greeted as close friends. The library director and his staff acted as if they had known everyone for a long time, their warmth and sincerity moving us to tears. Later, my friend and editor wrote about that meeting.

Vera Deinichenko, Journalist and Editor:
'Well, at last, my friend, Laureate of the Eurasian Creative Guild, Gulsifat Shahidi's books were received in the city of Suvorov. She came to the meeting herself along with her readers and a support group of Dushanbe residents. They

were Lyudmila Sinitsyna, a journalist, writer and photographer who visited me last summer, Nazokat Kholova, with whom we worked in the Union of Theatre Activists of Tajikistan, and her daughter Tanya. They were driven by my countryman, Farrukh Holmuradov, our faithful assistant in all matters from Moscow to Suvorov.

'The presentation took place in the Palace of Culture in the reading room of the regional library. The hostess, Nellja Sergeyevna Merkulova and the library's employees, Marina V. Zaytseva, Marina Nikolaevna Kharkova, Natalya Mikhailovna Bolushkova, Oksana Silaevna Silaeva and Olga Vasilyevna Goetze created an amazing atmosphere through their benevolence and kindness.

'I brought my Tajik dress made of khan-atlas fabric so that everyone could feel it, as well as a hand-coloured satin scarf made for me at the Fashion Theatre of the Centre for Creative Development and Humanitarian Education, the print of which had become the cover design for the book about Zhukovsky.

'The meeting opened with a piece of music by the world-famous composer, Tolib Shahidi, which he had composed for the film, *Go Forward, Guards!* I could not resist the temptation and started dancing a Tajik folk-dance. Then, the young correspondents and readers of Suvorov gave their impressions on the books written by Gulsifat Shahidi. Many of them very much liked Nekbakht, a character from the story, *The City Where Dreams Come True*, the guest worker Abdulvassi and the oligarch Gleb Nikolayevich Dobrov from *Farhod from Navgilem*, and cheerful and resilient Ly-

ubasha - for some reason, people noted her similarity to me
– the frontline soldier Grigori Semenovich, Farhod, Shirin
and Zulfiya from the novel, *My Neighbourhood Sisters*.

'How many words of gratitude the author heard! At
times, Gulsifat could not hide her tears of joy. She didn't
refuse to pen an autograph for anyone, writing dedications
and presenting her books to all.'

As the author, I was very pleased that so many school-
children and students came to this event. I was struck by
their faces - soulful, open, hearty and sincere. I immediately noted that the attendees were not coming across my
work for the first time, but had already read the books and
spoke about specific themes, characters and events described
in them. How wonderful the speeches at the meeting were,
two of which I wish to bring to your attention.

Daria Veselova, Student at the Tula Medical Institute:
'I really like the story by Gulsifat Shahidi, 'A Beauty
and Confucius' from the book, *My Neighbourhood Sisters*.
Its main character is Lyubov Vladimirovna, or Lyubasha, as
the author affectionately calls her. It seems to me that she
is very similar in character and some moments of her life
to Vera Vladimirovna Deinichenko, our journalism tutor,
and even their middle names are the same. For example,
let me recite: "Lyubasha amazed everyone with her cheer-
fulness, intelligence and kindness. She knew a lot of jokes,
knew how to tell them to an audience, and was reputed to
be easily amused. Lyubasha had a son, Sergey, who loved to

read and wrote poetry."

'I know that Vera Vladimirovna also has a son called Sergey who writes poems. The portrait description is also a 100% similar to Vera Vladimirovna: "She was short and very charming: a snub nose, fine white teeth and big blue eyes that fascinated me with their charm. She attended concerts and performances looking so beautiful that all the neighbours came out to see and appreciate her. Her blonde hair did not require any care and flowed over her shoulders in waves. She just had to comb it once and her hairstyle was ready as if she'd just exited a salon."

'I also liked the fact that there were so many wise sayings by the Chinese philosopher, Confucius in the story. Here are some of them:

"We accept tips in drops, but distribute them in buckets."

"If you hate, it means you are conquered."

"There is beauty in everything, but not everyone can see it."

'I want to extend my thanks to Gulsifat Gafforovna for giving me the opportunity to become acquainted with the Tajik people and their traditions.'

Inna Sycheva, Student of the Faculty of Philology of the Moscow Pedagogical University:

'In the new book by Gulsifat Gafforovna Shahidi, *Farhod from Navgilem*, I immediately made note of one of the characters, the oligarch Gleb Nikolayevich Dobrov. He is a decent and honest person who hires Tajik migrant workers and becomes for them a true friend and helper in life. In difficult moments he supports the three friends, Abdulvasi, Farhod and Faridun. Gleb Nikolayevich is able to defuse tension with jokes, cheering up everyone and defending his Tajik friends against attacks by skinhead scum. Therefore, the author has invented a self-explanatory surname, 'Dobrov' (meaning 'a kind person').

'This character brought to mind Vera Vladimirovna's husband, the poet Gleb Nikolayevich Deinichenko. I am not acquainted with him personally, but I know a lot about him from the stories of Vera Vladimirovna, from her book, *Letters to My Son*, and from the poems written by Gleb Nikolayevich. The guys at Yunkor (young correspondents) School have hosted evenings more than once at which his works were read aloud. They chose the literature themselves, and each of us found something of ourselves, some emotional experience in those verses. Here is one of his familiar poems, which I found in the pages of the book by Gulsifat Gafforovna, as read by the oligarch Dobrov:

> Kindness is always beautiful,
> It is not loud at all.
> Warm and sincere, merciful,
> This is its essence for all.
> You'd better let well enough alone,
> Wait from morning till the next morning.
> No one can buy for himself the good,
> Because it has one master - God.

'This poem by Gleb Nikolaevich Deinichenko is called "Dobro" (Kindness). It seems to me that it is close both to the character of the story and to the oligarch. After all, Gleb Nikolayevich, like the oligarch Dobrov, is a cheerful, kind, and sympathetic man.

'Now, I'd like to tell you about my correspondence acquaintance with Gulsifat Gafforovna. Last year, before entering the Faculty of Philology of the Moscow Pedagogical University, I built a page on the website 'proza.ru' and posted my first story, "A March to Victory" there. A few days later, I saw that Gulsifat Gafforovna had written a mini-review of it. It was very nice to read the writer's opinion about my work. It seems to me that everyone who starts writing wants to learn how to do it well, and it is important to hear the comments and get advice from intelligent people.'

So, this is how I came to visit the homeland of Vasily Andreyevich Zhukovsky again after 35 years. I found that his spirit is still alive and well, because to this day his countrymen continue to look towards the East.

COMMENTS AND REVIEWS

IF ONLY THERE WAS NO WAR
THE NOVEL 'ZAHHAK' BY V. MEDVEDEV

I love Tajikistan, a stunning land where the mountains embrace the clouds and kiss the sky. I love my compatriots, beautiful, proud, hard-working, patient and the kindest people on Earth. Therefore, I try to read everything that is written about my home country, especially books by people who have lived and worked with us to build a modern and prosperous Republic.

When I read the novel, *Zahhak*, I felt the pain of the author and his concern for the fate of his characters. Then I reread it, and both times it was difficult to recollect those events from thirty years ago. This book is not for the faint-hearted and the impression it leaves is very similar to watching the Iranian film, *The Stoning of Soraya M.* directed by Cyrus Nowrasteh. From its opening sentences, the book is stressful. War is always terrible, but when it is meaningless and self-destructive it is doubly so. Unfortunately, or perhaps fortunately, I can't comprehend how it this situation became possible, but as time passes a lot is forgotten.

This book is about the truth behind the brutal attacks of on simple, peaceful and sometimes naive people who cannot comprehend such cruelty. They also cannot understand the motives of thugs such as Zuhursho Khushkadam, the main villain of the novel and his friendship with a huge python, which he intimidates the villagers with, placing it around his neck. What can you expect from such a hard-hearted person? Thus, the inspiration for the title, *Zahhak*, is both derived from the word for snake and is a bloodthirsty ruler in the epic poem, *Shahnameh*, by Ferdowsi.

Medvedev discusses this idea in the novel: 'It is amazing how precise and, most importantly, how pertinent to modern times the image found in Ferdowsi is. The ruler is in symbiosis with reptiles, and together they consume the brains of his lieges. It is a brilliant metaphor which expresses the very essence of power. Violence is committed primarily against the minds of subordinates, and only secondarily upon their bodies.'

A character in the novel, Oleg, a journalist from Moscow states, 'it happens in Asia: robbers sometimes became rulers… Entire villages are massacred, eliminated with savage ingenuity.'

Intriguingly, the novel begins with the discovery of a skull at a construction site by Andrei, the son of Vera and Umar Murodov. It leads to the denouement of the narration, as the skull is the severed head of Zahhak. The author masterfully portrays the execution of Zahhak by Karim Tykva, a simple and trusting man, who by taking the life of the bloodthirsty murderers shows that by their actions such figures sentence themselves to the same cruel fate that they inflict.

Each chapter is the dramatic tale of one of the main characters in the novel: Andrei, Zarina, Dzhorub, Karim Tykva, Oleg, Davron and Eshon Wahhob. The author uses an effective technique alternating the narration between the male and female characters throughout the course of the book. The chapters are named after the character narrating them, all of whom are ill-fated. There is Zarina, an attractive, joyful free-spirited woman forced to be Zahhak's wife, she sets herself on fire to escape her loveless marriage. Davron is a government official who seeks justice and order and protects the Murudov family. He carries the badly burnt girl, Zarina to a wise woman in the village of Talhak. Afterwards, he is captured and ends up in a dungeon where he meets the dying Oleg, who has bravely captured on film the atrocities committed by Zahhak. The author intertwines the fates of all his characters in such a fashion.

Alongside the main characters, an ensemble of their friends, enemies, relatives and neighbours complete the cast, with the author usually explaining the meaning behind their names. Many geographical locations are also described, and their Tajik names and titles are translated into Russian. Medvedev's knowledge of Tajik does not come from textbooks, but is derived from his experience as a native speaker who understands proverbs, slang, songs, poems and even swear words. He has lived among Tajiks for many years; he knows the customs of the local population and this adds to the believability of his writing.

Medvedev quotes from verses by, Validdin Hirszoda, a poet well renowned in Darvaz. It is not clear if this is a direct translation, or whether this is the author's reinterpretation:

If jealous flames engulf an obedient Peri,
Be afraid of this maiden, both humans and beasts.

Another selection includes:
It's better dragging a chest filled with sand through the desert,
Than to carry woeful news to a mother about her son.

These are the violent and desperate lamentations of Bakhshanda over the body of her murdered husband:

Oh, my house, my house, four walls with no roof.
My king has left, a dutar is without a string,
A jug without water, a hamam without a body,
Oh, my house, my house, my house is empty.

If guests come, you won't get up, you won't say Salaam,
Your horse is waiting for you under the saddle.
In mid-summer, your cup is covered with ice,
Oh, my house, my house is all ruined.

In Tajik folklore, there is a tradition of female poetic lamentations using the refrain, '*be honumonam.*' Medvedev is aware of this and makes poignant use of it throughout the novel. His text is also sprinkled with proverbs and sayings, such as:

1.'If there had not been a nose between them, one eye would have pecked out the other.'

This is the Tajik proverb, '*Agar bini naboshad, yak chashm digar chashmro kofta megarad.*'

2. 'If you pull him by the nose, his soul will jump out of him.'

In Tajik, '*Az binniash giri chonash mebaroyad.*'

3. 'A crooked man has a crooked shadow.'

This is the translation of the Tajik proverb, '*Odami kachro soyaash ham kach meshavad.*'

4. 'There is only one roof, buy many types of weather.'

The Tajik equivalent, '*Yak bomu du havo.*'

The novel offers rich material for linguists, folklorists and local historians. With the names of villages, rivers, gorges and even road junctions, a map of the mountainous regions of Tajikistan is created. From Darvaz to Kalai Humba, the author mentions Talhak, Vaziron, Vorukh, Vatan, Darai Shur, Darai Gurgon, the Sarbiyon Mountains, the Hazrati Hussein range, the Yah-Su River and Osmon-Kul Lake.

From his rendition of events in the book, the impression is given that the author does not invent or exaggerate, but rather was witnessed the events moulded into fiction. One can even envisage him as the character of Oleg, a first-hand observer of that terrible war as encapsulated in this quote: 'I followed the events with horror, through newspapers, radio and television. One of my comrades, who had lived in Tajikistan for many years, after watching television reports, once exclaimed: "We have always believed that the Tajiks are amazingly beautiful people, gentle, friendly, hard-working and cheerful. Where have they gotten this pathological cruelty from? It turns out that they are not at all as they appeared..." "And you just summed up our civil war," I replied. "During cataclysms, sadists, psychopaths and born killers always come to light."'

I fully concur with Medvedev's sentiments here. His book is about remembering this meaningless confrontation and learning from it so it does not happen again. It was very difficult after the war; there was no bread, heat, and light. It was a world without men, who had died or left in search of work. Many suffered and yet, still believed that everything would be fine if only there was no war.

WHEN DREAMS COME TRUE

COMMENTS ON THE BOOK,
'AMINA TURAN IN THE COUNTRY OF NOMADS'
BY ZAURE TUREKHANOVA.

I want to congratulate Zaure Turekhanova, the author of *Amina Turan in the Country of Nomads*, published by Almatykitap Baspasi. It is both patriotic and original, containing a treasure-trove of Kazakh mythology and folklore.

Despite her youth, Zaure is an established author. The winner of prestigious prizes in Kazakhstan, she also won an award at a festival in London where we met for her book about Almaty. I observed her confident presentation on the subject, wherein she displayed excellent knowledge of research material on the ancient city. It was equally pleasing to see that she was supported by her charming mother, Zulfiya-Khanum.

At that time, Zaure informed me about her upcoming book, which was set to be published in Russian. For me, its title, *Amina Turan in the Country of Nomads*, brings to mind *Alice's Adventures in Wonderland*. In the book – dedicated to her beloved grandfather, Moldagali Berdjanov –Zaure sets out to convey all the beauty of Kazakh mythological epic literature and folklore.

The book is an easy read, albeit rather long for its intended audience. Children may find it difficult to absorb in one sitting, but the fascinating style of the tale will see them return. The lead character, Amina, is a lovely twelve-year-old girl with strength and wisdom an adult would envy. Every new test Amina encounters is part of a path that will lead to the happiness of her people, especially those who are in despair and rely on her courage and ingenuity. Each chapter is a new adventure for her, as evinced by the character, Idahar Campire, who explains: 'I will send a test to measure her willpower and the kindness of her heart. If she is the one whom we need, then the girl, no doubt, is the one for this mission, and this means that she will cope with any task.'

Through her characters, the author proclaims eternal truths, such as: 'After all, you need to look not at age, but at what is in the soul and the conscience of a person,' and, 'If this girl has a desire to do good and help people, the mythic characters will give her a chance by testing her in practice and believing in her nobility. Her every journey is a new challenge.'

With her kind and sympathetic heart, the brave girl manages to overcome her many obstacles, including a genie, a black sorcerer, the giants of Zardakhsha, and Karga the sorceress. In the end, Amina fulfils her mission, finds the Book of Fates and saves the inhabitants of the city.

Through her characters, Zaure explains the circle of karmic justice in this quote from the novel, 'As you know, if you do good it comes back to you with added strength, and if you do evil, then that evil will return to you fiercer than before.'

The story is permeated with an appreciation and deep love of Kazakh history, mythology and folktales. Although this fantasy is intended for children, it is a work which adults can also learn from and enjoy. Zaure perfectly sums up the themes in her novel when she states, 'Dreams come true when you believe in them and strive for perfection.'

'THAT'S ALL.
THERE WILL BE NO MOVIE.'

NOTES ON THE BOOK,
'THE FILMS OF BAKO SADYKOV,'
BY MUKHIDDIN MAKHMUDOV.

With regards to this book, I recall the words of a major character from the film, *Gentlemen of Fortune*, 'That's all. There will be no Movie.' Many films produced before the period of 'Reconstruction,' or, as the author describes it, in the era of timelessness were doomed to 'shelf-oblivion.' A great deal of money, technical and human resources were spent making a movie only for it to be placed in an archive, never to be seen.

Time demonstrates that great films will eventually find their audience. After reading Makhmudov, I concluded that Bako Sadykov, despite obstacles, barriers and misunder-

standings, is still a happy person. He expresses his ideas and creates beautiful masterpieces with a specific Sufi flavour. Obviously, there might be objections that the author is a faithful friend of Sadykov and, therefore, the portrayal in this book is biased. I'm not a film critic and these are purely my personal observations, but fans and colleagues should be allowed to write about creative persons that inspire them; it is their right.

Bako Sadykov was in no way ordinary. It is not always easy to understand the language of his movies. His first film, *Adonis the XIV*, which was 'completely under arrest during the last ten years,' left no one indifferent. In my opinion, this was a fable about human vanity conveyed through symbolism. This was the director's vision; he was not looking for simple solutions and his subsequent work would be further proof of that. As the film expert, Lutfiya Aini explained, 'It has the flavour of an old parable.' Sadykov was fascinated by Sufism, inspired by the works of such Sufi poets as Rumi, Sanoi and Attor.

Before writing this review, I searched for Bako Sadykov online, a new habit I've gradually acquired. Google contained only fourteen pages worth of publications, articles and reviews on the life and work of the director. I found a list of all his films on Wikipedia and Film Site, whilst YouTube only had something on *Adonis the XIV*.

In his book, Makhmudov brings together a collection of articles, interviews, librettos, screenplays and letters from Sadykov's archives. Despite the large amounts of research and documentary material included in the text, it is easy to navigate, though it probably will require more than one sitting. The book is designed for a wide range of readers and will prove to be of special interest to colleagues and specialists in the history of Soviet and post-Soviet cinema.

I'm grateful to the author for giving me this book, otherwise, I doubt I would of have found it. Even though I rarely go back to my homeland, I still like to read everything about the region, especially when it concerns people who are involved in the development and promotion of Tajik art on an international level.

Makhmudov describes his subject with deep respect and concern, rejoicing in his successes and creative endeavours whilst also lamenting the lack of understanding and occasional rejection of his work. Here the author quotes from an article by G. Rakhmatov about the film, *The Blessed Bukhara*: 'Oriental people have accepted that film enthusiastically, because it reflects the fate of the nation. However, it is rather tortuous, like the streets of Bukhara, but not hopeless. After each street, there is a new passage. You might think that it's the end of the world, everything is a dead end, but suddenly a new opening and other transitions appear. And the person, having sighed with relief, opens for himself a new world. And so on without end. If one sees building material in a brick, another person perceives it as a tool for striking; Bako Sadykov sees a handful of ancestral land in it.' (*Adabiet va Sanat* (Literature and Art) June 13th, 1991)

In collecting such a wealth of material on the director, Makhmudov embraces the immensity of his subject. There is enough here that it could easily have been published in

several books, yet it is squeezed into four hundred pages of succinct and encyclopaedic detail without an excessive degree of clutter.

Creative and talented people are always surrounded not only by admirers, colleagues and friends, but also by critics. Without this sense of opposition or obstacle, there is no art. I can attest to this from my own personal experience of being the wife of a famous and talented composer and through my own creative endeavours. Whilst the gossip and envy of others can be detrimental, it can also harden our reserve and make us stronger.

Conventions and adherence to the status quo may hold back an idea, like a bird in a cage, but eventually, it will find its way to freedom and soar high amongst the clouds. To encapsulate the above sentiments, I'd like to conclude this chapter with a Sufi parable written by Rumi.

THE MERCHANT AND THE PARROT

A merchant known for his talking parrot was to travel to Hindustan on business. Before he set out, he asked his children and other household members what presents each of them would like to receive from that distant land. After they had expressed what they would like, the merchant asked his parrot for what he would desire.

'When you arrive in my fatherland, tell all the parrots of Hindustan that I am tormented by my separation from them. That I constantly think about them in my imprisonment, and I am waiting for their advice on how to cope with my sorrow. After all, my multi-coloured dear beloved lives there too. We were like Layla and Majnun, and I remember her with love. May she, on having received this message, remember me, and let her shed a tear in memory,' the parrot answered.

The merchant vowed to fulfil the request of the parrot. When he arrived in Hindustan, he saw many happy birds there and immediately remembered his oath, accurately conveying the parrot's words to his compatriots. When he finished his story, one of the parrots loudly squawked and fell dead, spreading his weakened wings. The merchant immediately felt guilty for this, and for a long time after scolded himself for relaying the parrot's sentiments so precisely.

His business venture came to a conclusion, and with the gifts he had promised he made his way back. When he returned, the parrot was waiting for him.

'Have you run my errand?' asked the parrot.

'I have done what you asked, but now I regret it. As soon as I told the birds how you were languishing here, one of them was so upset that it fell down dead. Neither I nor the other birds could help it,' the merchant lamented.

Upon hearing that story, the parrot dropped his head and fell to the bottom of his gilded cage. He fluttered his wings and then froze in a similar fashion to his deceased kinsman from Hindustan. Grief-stricken by the death of his bird, the merchant tore off his turban and began tearing off his clothes.

'Your voice was so sweet! Why have you done this to

yourself? Shall I never hear your singing and your speeches again? Can I not bring you back to life? After all, birds like you have never been known, even in the gardens of King Solomon,' he wailed in despair.

The merchant spent the whole day in such anguish and only by the evening did he manage to calm down. He then carried the cage into the garden, carefully took the bird into his hands and laid him out. Suddenly, the parrot came to life, opened his eyes and flew up onto a branch.

The merchant couldn't believe his eyes.

'How did you come up with this trick? Have I without knowing it brought the advice of your brethren from Hindustan to you?' he wailed.

'You've brought a message from my brothers to me,' the parrot explained. 'They told me that I should stop pleasing people with my singing, because the louder and more melodious it is, the stronger my cage will be. My brother advised me to feign my death in order to find freedom. Goodbye, my master, I will never forget that I am free thanks to you.'

The merchant mulled over what the parrot had said.

'May the Lord protect you, for by your actions you have brought me closer to understanding of the truth. Thank you for the lesson. Goodbye, and fly to your true love,' replied the merchant.

I would like to conclude my reflections with an extract from Sadykov's letter to the journalist, Tamara Khetaguro-va: 'Life goes on. I am inspired in this life by my interest in everything that surrounds me, my beloved Zubeida, my

sons, grandchildren and daughter-in-law.'

Therein lies the secret to true happiness, which Makhmudov's book reflects.

DILYARA LINDSAY:
'I LEARNT TO TRUST THE SOUND'

Meet the new name in the world of literature: Dilyara Lindsay. Her collection of poems and short stories, *Music Between the Lines* has just been published. A truly Eurasian author, she is a Kazakh born in Tashkent, Uzbekistan, living in London and writing in Russian.

I have known the author for several years. At one of my presentations in London, she gave me her reviews of my books, *The City Where Dreams Come True* and *My Neighbourhood Sisters*. Dilyara did not just express her impressions of my works, but also provided a correct and objective analysis of the images, characters and situations, noting the accessibility of the language which enabled readers to easily understand the style and figurative nature of the texts.

When I was asked to review the first book by Dilyara, I agreed without hesitation. Though she is a novice author, she has been writing for many years, honing her creative abilities whilst plagued by doubts. Her work, though, is an unreserved success. I noticed immediately that she is modest in expressing the images of poetic lyrics and does not claim to be among the stars. Emotions are felt, sometimes leading to an unpredictable pathos and sometimes to an incompatibility of size or rhyme, but it is clear that the author does this on purpose knowing that she cannot replace or change her thoughts. It is sincere, and sincerity overcomes a lot.

Dilyara dedicates the collection of poems and prose to her 'beloved parents,' to her only son, the 'Man of the New Time,' and to her late spouse, 'who has left this world too soon.' She writes in the preface: 'I belong to the generation of people who, by the will of fate, have witnessed the collapse of a huge Soviet realm. In the "before" period, there was a happy, bright childhood and a long, 21-year-long musical education.'

It was not at random that I chose that passage, but because I realised that music, despite all the twists and turns of fate, remains a fundamental chain in the life and work of Dilyara Lindsay. It is because of this that she named her book, *Music Between the Lines*. Both the poems and the author's stories are full of sound; music is heard in them:

> All taken by the desire to discover
> The law of Godlike harmony,
> I learnt to trust the sound
> And hear other souls' symphonies...

Dilyara looks at life as a musician. Although she changed her profession long ago, she remains eternally grateful to music:

Many secrets are being revealed to me gradually:
That every person represents an instrument.
In the large orchestra of mortal life,
                                    he's playing fatefully,
He's given his own melody and moment.

Due to her professional music education, Dilyara admits that she has been formed as an individual personality, learnt to think and feel organically, figuratively, and on a large scale. Even true love she learnt throughout the art of music:

Music has brought us together,
With a pattern of notes covering my road;
The star of love is lit with chords forever,
And this has led to your soul's threshold.

The author's attitude towards her creative undertaking is very responsive, and she freely admits that she is not striving to be original. She is very modest and unpretentious, simply looking for an outlet for her tender feelings:

All the great poets are already published,
All the best songs are probably composed.
But my hand is drawn still to write sonnets,
To rhyme the words of love like those poets.
Discover in yourself a source of inspiration,
In the labyrinth of fate, you'll find fascination.
Search for yourself without hesitation,
Believe in universal love's predomination.

Dilyara Lindsay's prose differs from her poetry in its factual nature, exploring local lore and autobiographical material. It is not academic, but a creative attempt by the author to articulate about her travels.

The first story is called 'The Jailoo of Eternal Pioneers.' A *jailoo* is a camp for nomads, the parts of whom are played by the 'eternal pioneers,' a group of romantic friends. Konstantin, the main instigator and organiser, annually holds the Zarniytsa festival of the soul with his large family and a group of friends. Having taken place for so many years, the departure to a yurt in August has become a tradition: 'In order to get drunk on the clear mountain air once again and to "poison" yourself in a good way on the indescribable beauty and grace of the Altai meadows and be filled with the powerful charge of luxurious human communication under the arches of the capricious Tian Shan sky.' Again, a musical reference concludes the tale:

'All good things come to an end, and now the final day of the summer holidays has arrived. As far back as I can remember, this day is always bright, sunny and special. It is as the finale of a major symphony, loudly summarising all that has passed.'

The story is told by the author in such a manner that you believe everything said and experience all the moments of her summer tale, which are enough to fuel an entire year, with her.

The second story is entitled, 'Odyssey of Senior Salazar, or The Adventures of an English Nomad.' This reads like an excerpt from Dilyara Lindsay's biography, and is a

happy tale as evinced by the tone of its narrator. The story is set in the post-musical stage of the author's life, the period when music turned into the poetry and prose of her life in Kazakhstan, South Africa and England. The author and the main character turn out to be similar, somehow even the same people:

'Later, when we began to wander together,' he loved to repeat:

"My life is a real adventure without a finale. I would never change what I have for a settled, regular life... Vacations? What do you mean? My whole life is a vacation. All I do is travel and enjoy life!"'

Many passages in Dilyara's book are devoted to the biography of its hero: who he is, where does he come from and who are his relatives? How did he start travelling and become a polyglot, learning so many languages? The author describes how they met and began to study their land and people together; and with what love it is described, especially the final moments before parting with the beloved forever. This, one must read for oneself. It is impossible to retell; one must feel it:

'At that moment, to the sounds of her favourite music, Salazar's bright soul was carried away to the fabulous paradise of his childhood where it will live forever, bathing in the tender rays of the ever-golden sun among tiny fairy-tale hummingbirds and the redolent scent of blooming orange alleys...'

I am certain that the poetry and prose of the truly Eurasian writer Dilyara Lindsay will find a place in the hearts of

many readers. In many ways, her first book, *Music Between the Lines* is an experiment, but there will be many more books, I'm sure of it.

'THE TAJIKS ARE COMING'
BY UMED BABAKHANOV

I thought long and hard about what to call my review of the book by Umed Babakhanov published in 2012 by the Er-graf Publishing House in Dushanbe, before deciding to leave the title as it is: *The Tajiks are Coming.* How many connotations there are in this title; and although it is taken from a single article, it is well suited to the entire collection. The Tajiks of the author's work spread out across the vast expanse of the Earth, conquering the hearts of millions in the process. These are the people of Tajikistan, a unique country which has passed through many travails. Its people remained unchanged, however: kind, hospitable, with a worldview shaped by centuries of tradition. And the same can be said of the author, who describes even the most terrible chapters in the modern history of Tajikistan very objectively. Intelligence is the main character trait in Babakhanov's writing, and it has deep roots.

There is a wise saying in the Tajik language: '*Merosi padar hohey, kasbi padar omuz*,' which translates as 'If you want to inherit your father's wealth, learn his profession.' Dedicating his book to his father, teacher and friend, Mansur, Umed Babakhanov is a living embodiment of this wisdom.

I knew Umed's father, a famous historian, political scientist and researcher. I was consistently amazed by his rich intelligence and ability to speak very calmly on any subject without unnecessary emotion. He knew how to listen and, without imposing his opinion, explain and reason out loud in order to convince his interlocutor. This was his talent. Calling everything by its name, Mansur Babakhanov did not tolerate empty disputes. No one could ever leave his company offended or dissatisfied, whatever their temperament. He left a lot of good works for us, but the main wealth of his life was his children, Umed and Firuza.

Why do I share these recollections about Mansur Babakhanov? Because reading this book by his son, it was as if I felt his presence. His intelligence has clearly been transmitted to Umed, both as a man and as a journalist. Given his lineage, how could Umed fail but become a talented writer? According to polling, the Asia-Plus Media Group with which he started his distinguished career has been amongst the most popular news sources in Tajikistan for many years.

Umed Babakhanov studied to be an orientalist and, as he confesses, 'never planned to become a journalist.' With outstanding skill as a translator, as one of the top graduates of the Faculty of Oriental Studies at the Tajik State University, he had excellent prospects in the diplomatic field. Having

taken the opportunity to work in the diplomatic corps in the Middle East, Umed then chose a different path. Perestroika gave him his wings. He believed in everything new and decided to return to Tajikistan in that 'beautiful and naive time.' Accepting a posting as a correspondent for the republican newspaper, *Komsomolets Tajikistana*, Umed soon understood that he had found his way. More than 25 years later, with each new piece he pens, he continues to prove that he chose the right path.

Opening this collection, it immediately became clear to me why Umed had elected to start with the article, 'The Tajiks are Coming,' a piece which gives impetus to the entire book. The older generation of Tajiks readers will remember an initiative by Munira Nabiyeva, a student of the Dushanbe Pedagogical Institute, to create a virtual 'Belt around the World' on the 39th parallel on which Tajikistan is located. Noting that other countries such as Greece, Italy, Spain, the United States and North Korea are situated in the same belt, Munira proposed that we 'make friends in our mutual house' and live in peace. As the author confesses, 'Perestroika was a very naive epoch.'

Although all of the republics had to go through a painful transitional period, the years following the collapse of the Soviet Union hit Tajikistan in the hardest way possible. Because of this, the author devotes four weighty chapters to this topic: 'The Premonition of Trouble,' 'The Chronicle of Madness,' 'A Business Trip to Afghanistan' and 'A War.' The titles of the articles aptly summarise everything written about the conflict in Tajikistan: 'Some Shoot, Others Leave,'

'Wherever You Look there is Blood,' 'Probably We have Gone Mad,' 'Don't Touch My House, I'll be Back,' 'Whilst Walking around Dushanbe, Beware of Militants,' 'Elephants Quietly Die in Zoos,' 'The Branches of Power Grow from the Barrel of a Machine Gun,' and others. At that troubled time, Umed Babakhanov was already an experienced journalist, a special correspondent for *Komsomolskaya Pravda* and a witness to everything that occurred. Writing about refugees who had crossed the border to Afghanistan, the author quotes the words of his hero: 'If there is a Day of Last Judgment, then we have already seen it.'

Independence came to Tajikistan through severe trials. As the author comments: 'the Tajik word "*ozodi*" (freedom) turned out to have a salty taste, the taste of tears and blood.' With faith in the victory of reason, Umed rejoices in the signing of the peace treaty which ended the Civil War. He names this chapter: 'New Age, New Hopes and New Disappointments.' Here, I would highlight the author's question, 'Do we need repentance?' as the core motif. He is right in believing it is necessary to correct errors, to understand each other better and to be on the alert so as to eradicate the threat of another fratricidal war and create a new Tajikistan. The task of building roads and bridges, tunnels and hydroelectric power stations was indeed an onerous one.

Umed Babakhanov has visited many countries: Russia, Kazakhstan, Afghanistan, the Czech Republic, China, Japan, England, Switzerland, Germany, South Korea; I could go on, but my point is that reading his articles about his travels one quickly reaches the conclusion that he has a fine

grasp of international politics. His convincing assessments, restrained criticism, moderate pathos and evidence-based conclusions are worthy of an experienced diplomat. He is well-versed in all that he describes; his unfestooned text is easy to follow and quickly wins the trust of the reader.

Personally, I am not a political animal. I don't like politics and do not have time for the chicanery involved. For a long time, politics has been called 'controlled chaos,' and analysts and journalists have discussed this axiom, but it transpires that because of those in the seats of power it is very difficult for anything to be achieved. No, politics is not for me, but Umed Babakhanov writes about it with awareness of the problems.

In the article, 'Democrats of All Countries, Unite' about the International Forum in Seoul, the author calls the Forum 'a big party' for the representatives of the world's major democracies. As a citizen, however, he is concerned by the question, 'who will determine which country is a developing democracy and which is sliding back towards dictatorship?'

As a member of government delegations, Umed Babakhanov has been a participant at several summits aimed at fostering cooperation and establishing closer diplomatic relations. He tells of his experiences modestly, without focusing attention on himself. Everything is restrained in his narration. He 'cuts a window to Europe' with President Emomali Rahmon and members of the delegation visiting France, describing in detail Rahmon's meeting with Jacques Chirac. From France, the delegation flies onto America, where they convene with representatives of the business community in meetings which the author calls historic. Further on, there are visits to Belgium and Germany, but in every case the main issue for the author is the drive for cooperation and the implementation of mutual interests.

There are also academic articles in the book, amongst which I would like to highlight the study, 'The Reform of the Tajik Writing System,' in which the author meticulously outlines the process of the triple transition of the Tajik alphabet from Arabic to Latin, and then from Latin to Cyrillic. The author gives examples of the complexity of the Chinese and Japanese alphabets, noting that despite this neither China or Japan has changed their written language. The Tajiks, however, have changed their letters with an Arabic heritage, allegedly because of their complexity, an issue affecting the literacy rate of the people. Umed cites many examples from the history of the Tajik language, expressing his regret that already several generations of our compatriots cannot read the rich Tajik-Persian literature and historical sources in their original language, a fact with which I wholeheartedly agree.

The book also contains a plethora of interviews with interesting people to which the author adds quotes and statements by Tajik poets and writers including Sadriddin Ayni, the founder of Tajik-Soviet literature. I was particularly attracted by an interview with the famous German orientalist, Manfred Lorenz, whose works about the Tajik language and literature are popular in European research circles. Other interlocutors include such famous personalities as George Soros, Ahmadsho Masud, M. Peshkov, the Russian Ambas-

sador to Tajikistan, Davlat Hudonazarov, the filmmaker, Valery Ahadov, and the writer, Timur Zulfikarov.

All of the interviews are unfailingly interesting and informative. To quote from the article, 'The Ant of Varzob Gorge' dedicated to the 70th birthday of the famous writer, Timur Zulfikarov: 'They call him the most Christian and the most Muslim, the most erotic and the most ascetic of men. "My literature is like wild grapes," Timur Kasymovich says of his work, "intrinsically sweet and without any chemicals."' I particularly enjoyed Zulfikarov's statements about fate: 'Man has come from Paradise, and he is going back there. Great meek persons go to Heaven. Hell is only on Earth… A real poet is always lonely, but any lonely sage is always waiting and listening should anyone knock at his door.'

It is an impossible thing to retell all that is good and wise about Umed Babakhanov's collection of articles. *The Tajiks are Coming* simply must be read. It has been published as a limited edition and is being transferred from hand to hand. I wish the author great success in his creative endeavours. I believe in his gift for writing.

A JUG OF FEMALE MELODIES
BY RAUSHAN

A new book by Raushan Burkitbaeva-Nukenova, *Curls of Karaculs* has arrived through the Moscow Publishing House, Khudozhestvennaya Literatura which represents her selected writings. As noted by the editor of the collection, the academic and director of the publishing house, Georgy Pryakhin: 'I haven't read anything more revealing, sensual and tragic in modern oriental female poetry for a long time.'

Poetry is the suspension of enchanted dreams.
A poetry critic will value these caught strange beams.

There is a Tajik proverb, '*Ismash ba chismash muvofik,*' which translates as: 'The name corresponds to the internal and external appearance of a person.' There are people who, over the course of the years, change so they no longer correspond to their name at all, but not Raushan, whose name

is derived from the Tajik word, '*Ravshan*' meaning 'light, bright and radiant,' and in some contexts 'open, warm and understanding.' Her parents named her well, for Raushan radiates light to everyone and is unceasing in her warmth.

Thanks to translations of her work, the award-winning Russian speaking Kazakh poet, Raushan Burkitbaeva-Nukenova will already be familiar to readers in many countries. In some ways, we are similar. I also write in Russian, often on the theme of love for my native land, my people, relatives, friends, and my nearest and dearest. A shared longing is clear, but Raushan is a poet who notices everything and sometimes sees beyond it:

...When a hail of memories
Harshly break your heart at once,
Extract from your subconscious
A fall into an abyss.

Down below the pass,
A stormy river rushes in extension,
Where so much joy and affection
A gentle hand presented in the past.

A doctor by profession and a healer through her poetry, Raushan is multifaceted in her work, but the key thing is its sound. Sometimes fervent and joyful, but mostly an intimate ostinato, it is both thoughtful and sad. These are the sounds we all heard from our elders when they sang us lullabies:

Don't break my soul, don't...
Through the cries on the crowded streets,
I will break through the bars of fences
And because of the bright light, I shall blink.

The pure sounds of music, shortly,
Will twang from beyond the screen,
Waves of sound will flood through the parting
Into the dry neck of a fountain.

In many ways, the poetry of the Central Asia countries is similar in its themes and plots, its polyphony and its vibrant colours. Perhaps only those who have visited the beautiful and extraordinary corners of Central Asia and seen the land of mighty mountains and vast expanses unlike other countries will truly comprehend the music of Raushan's verses:

The music of Aethyr is heard in the oppressive silence...
The chime of night has been leading to the depths.

The title of one of Raushan's collections of poems is *The Music of Lines*, and in this selected works you can hear music everywhere. Such is the case in 'A Moonlight Sonata,' a poem dedicated to Beethoven:

You filled us with your perfect creation untiringly,
Like light piercing through darkness, an immortal man.

Raushan writes about Bach:
The fruitful father wrote many masses and fugues,
Into a musical chest, he placed a prelude cycle for blizzards.

Of Brahms *Hungarian Dance* she writes:

And the people started dancing to the sounds...
And all this is the music of Paradise

Silently leaving the depths of the box,
In embraces of freedom and darkness,
Music wanders the suburbs in silence
And resounds through the tunnel of emptiness.

The music of Raushan's poetry is full of love, feelings and desires, but also a bright, translucent sense of melancholy. Everyone can empathise with the flame of love and the tender sadness which accompanies it. Except in fairytales and humorous novels, there is no love without sadness. In life, everything is more serious.

There's no better friend than a snowstorm,
One can open one's heart to it
About the beloved man, be melancholy and mourn;
We shall howl together for a while.

But sadness and longing do not only bring sorrow. Sadness is light and gives warmth. To speak frankly about life as it truly is can teach us a lot:

> I can't forget the happy moment
> When the fragrant plum-tree scent
> Filled my stuffy study-room.
> Alas, you have not stayed with me forever,
> Only the bloom of your perfume remains.

Raushan accepts love with a smile, always honest, open and filled with the wisdom she has learnt from V. Bryusov, K. Balmont, I. Brodsky, O. Mandelstam, B. Pasternak, A. Akhmatova, B. Akhmadullina and Olzhas Suleymenov. Raushan does not sit still in the same place; she is an eternal wanderer. In her poems, you walk with her through her native village, in Chimbulak or in beautiful, picturesque Kok Tobe. As we travel around the world - Samarkand, Moscow, London, St. Petersburg, Paris - according to the poet's opinion, 'we are all foreigners in our own house.'

> Children go to the West, and we go to the East.
> In different places, we are looking for resources.

Where does fate carry us? What roads are destined for us? How will the universe dispose of us? In response, Raushan quotes Lev Gumilyov: 'In each of us there resides a genetic memory that is not felt in everyday life, but sometimes flashes in our subconscious.' Raushan answers these words with questions:

Where is fate carrying you?
A voodoo priest, will he prompt you into something?
The Ulba River runs to the Irtysh,
And the Milky Way will show your path.

The glassy world is so brittle,
No harder than a mammoth's body.
The feasts of this universe are so little,
The unseen sword of God hangs over us.

As Dünebek Nakipov writes in the preface of the book: 'Although Raushan, like all of us, lives with everyday anxieties and the problems posed by the differently tuned orchestras of the modern world, she resists harsh notes of censure. She conducts her search for lost harmony; her inner creed is the music of hope.'

I can only highly recommend that you read this book which gifts us the music of love, dreams, turmoil and hope.

BRAVO MEGAN! OR AN OLD HEAD ON YOUNG SHOULDERS

'The future belongs to those who believe in the beauty of their dreams.'
Eleanor Roosevelt

At the age of thirteen, Megan Werner wrote the book, *It's Up to Me: Seven Ways to Make a Difference*, which has already gone into its second imprint. A girl from Krugesdorp, South Africa, whilst still attending secondary school she put down on paper her dream that people could change for the better and make the world around them more beautiful.

When one reads the authors of pedagogical science such as Michel de Montaigne, Jan Amos Kaminsky or Dale Carnegie, one immediately feels their life experience. How does this 13-year-old girl have so many examples of daily practices to follow and reach such wise conclusions? One

must wonder not only at what is written, but also how it is written.

Megan is not trying to flaunt her intelligence; she is natural and sincere. Any thesis presented in her book vividly comes to life through examples from her memories, the books she has read and her life experiences. Yes, experience. Megan's parents and her sister are always nearby. They are her teachers in life and tell her how to find the right path and change situations for the better.

The ten chapters of this book present the life of a girl, where each sentence describing her memorable moments and even chapter headings can become dictums. I do not sing the praises of this young author lightly, but cannot help but express my delight as a reader. I will give just a few examples, although the whole book is written in such a surprisingly sagacious and at the same time simple and understandable style. Megan begins the book with words of gratitude, an emotion with which the whole book is infused. Here are the titles of some chapters:

'It is Noble to Share with Your Loved Ones'
'Never Listen to Pessimists'
'Tell Me Who Your Friend is and I Will Tell You Who You Are'

The entire book is a collection of thoughts which are not intrusive or abstruse, but suitable to life. Often Megan's words feel like you might have said them yourself or heard them somewhere before:

'Look for reasons to smile every day, even if sometimes it seems difficult.'

'Do not focus on the negative side of things.'

'It is very important to have an example to follow; if you strive after this ideal, inspiration will not leave you.'

'The future belongs to those who believe in the beauty of their dreams.'

'We must learn to use our gifts and talents, and to share them with others.'

'Even if you are tired of failure, do not give up!'

'Be as extraordinary as you can.'

'You progress only when you are out of your comfort zone.'

Each of these short phrases and sayings is cited, everything demonstrated with examples from the life of the author. The narration is also supplemented with stories from the lives of contemporaries and the legends of ancestors.

And what are these seven ways to change life for the better that Megan offers up? I shall give the answer with these short focal points which I have drawn from her book:

1. The reflection effect. Smile and the world will smile with you.

2. The sense of satisfaction. Positive energy is contagious.

'Do not let sadness from the past and fear of the future destroy happiness in the present.'

3. Courage. Here, Megan quotes her hero, Nelson Mandela: 'I learned that courage was not the absence of fear, but the triumph over it.'

4. Self-development and self-education are wonderful ways to improve your life and the lives of others for the better.

5. Teaching others: 'If you give a man a fish he is hungry again in an hour. If you teach him to catch a fish, you do him a good turn.'

6. Beneficence. One person cannot change the world, but everyone can try.

7. Learn to listen and to be grateful. If you are grateful for the little things in life, soon you will get much more. The main thing is to go through life with a lively sense of gratitude.

Megan Werner closes her book with a beautiful story:

'An old Chinese man who lived in the mountains was known for his wisdom. People from all over the world came to him for advice.

Once, a teenager decided to test the old man. He caught a butterfly. He had a plan: On having arrived with a living butterfly in his hands, he would to ask the old man whether it was alive or dead. If the elder answered, "alive," he would

crush the butterfly, and if he answered, "dead," he would let the butterfly go free.

"Sir, is the butterfly that is in my hands alive or dead?" he asked the elder.

After a pause, the old man responded:

"The answer, my son, is only in your hands."'

This is also true when it comes to our lives.

Megan Werner does not say goodbye to her readers, concluding her book with the words: 'Until we meet again, dear friends, continue to change life for the better!' I advise everyone to read this book. Sometimes the thoughts of children can amaze adults with their seemingly naive wisdom, but this wisdom makes us spiritually richer.

CRYING SILENTLY AND PRAYING TO GOD…

A REVIEW OF THE BOOK, 'CRANE' BY ABU-SUFYAN

'Only a mother can pray like that for her children.' These words written by the poet from Dagestan, Abu-Sufyan are very dear to me. He is also a child of the mountains with an oriental temperament who writes in Russian. I was touched by his attitude towards his mother; according to the canons of the Sacred Book, 'look for paradise under the feet of mothers.'

When the poet talks about life he does not seek to indoctrinate but to share with young people his love of Mother Nature and ability to treat all living things with care. I especially enjoyed the three poems: 'A Young She-Crane,' 'A Mare,' and the modern ballad, 'Mother.' We feel the pain of the author in these pieces, his experiences told through the stories of a mother-crane and a mother-mare. Their "destinies" echo the fate of human mothers who 'live alone, left by their children.' The author even calls the young she-crane by a gentle feminine name, 'Roza' (a rose). In difficult circumstances, this strong and beautiful bird does not abandon her only son, but fights for his life and wins:

> They flew away, flapping their wings,
> Rosa with her crane chick left, at last...
> Let misfortune touch them no more by any means,
> Protect them, O Creator, let them last.

In the poem, 'Mare,' at the expense of her own life, a mother saves her foal from thirst. She does everything to continue her kind; only a mother is capable of this:

> The long road collects dust:
> A mare runs on a trail,
> Her foal is running after her.
> Their road is long under a hot sun.

The prayers of mothers are always aimed at the well-being of their children, even those who have left them in their dotage. They live alone, waiting on the roads where they used to accompany their children:

> And idling away the time,
> In the captivity of dreams,
> She sits alone, almost blind,
> Losing ties with the world, so wide.

Despite all the insults and endless waiting, a mother still prays for her adult child even though 'her son has left for far away, easily leaving his home.' She, offended by fate, still hopes for his return:

She is crying silently and praying to God
To guard her son from evil.

A poet of immense talent, the work of Abu-Sufyan is suitable for both children and adults. I see in his poems many parallels with the parables of classical Tajik-Persian literature. In his images of birds and animals, the characteristic features of humans are easily recognised. His poems are informative and instructive. The spirit of the wisdom of the East prevails in them.

ГУЛЬСИФАТ ШАХИДИ

«НАСТОЯЩИЙ РАЙ ПОТЕРЯННЫЙ РАЙ»

Избранные статьи, отзывы и интервью

ШТРИХИ К ПОРТРЕТУ

«Настоящий рай – потерянный рай» – так назвала свой публицистический сборник лауреат премии Евразийской творческой гильдии писательница Гульсифат Шахиди. Это десятая по счёту книга моей подруги и землячки, увидевшая свет в московском издательстве «Перо».

Потерянный рай для нас обеих – самый лучший на свете город Душанбе – столица несравненного Таджикистана. Новая книга Гульсифат – дань памяти нашей молодости и первых шагов в журналистике в молодёжной газете «Комсомолец Таджикистана», творческим попыткам найти себя в освоении жанров очерка, интервью, рецензий. Мы искали свой стиль изложения, истово верили тогда, что каждый человек, с которым нас свела судьба, уникален, интересен и многому нас научит.

Вступительную статью к новому сборнику я назвала «Штрихи к портрету», и читатель увидит, как Гульсифат штрихами-жанрами рисует портрет нашего поколения, а по сути, портрет родного Таджикистана. Обратите внимание, какие острые и волнующие вопросы задаёт в интервью автор-журналист своим земляками, насколько искренние ответы получает от собеседников. Как профессионал уверяю вас, не всякому журналисту собеседник готов открыть душу и поделиться сокровенным. А у Гульсифат беседа строится на обоюдном доверии. Вот эти герои интервью – политик и Государственный советник юстиции Гульчехра Шарипова – «Женщина с сильным характером», фотохудожник Геннадий Ратушенко – патриот и пропагандист культуры Таджикистана во всём мире – «Фото – зрительская память истории», первая и единственная женщина-композитор на Памире Заррина Миршакар – «Прелюдия Навруза», художник-монументалист Муриват Бекназаров, считающий памирские горы величием мира – «Я горец, и этим всё сказано».

Эти интервью, опубликованные в «Вечёрке» в 1999–2006 годах, и сегодня поражают мощью характеров и творческих идей собеседников Гульсифат.

Гражданская братоубийственная война 90-х годов разбросала таджикистанцев по всему миру. Гульсифат почти два десятилетия живёт на две страны и на два города – в Москве и Лондоне. Именно в Лондоне ей пришла мысль собрать в единую книгу журналистские публикации и телепередачи, сделанные в период работы в таджикском филиале МГТРК «МИР». Мы обе плакали над повестью «Город, где сбываются мечты»: Гуля – как автор вновь переживала страшные события, а я – редактор очевидец тех лет противоборства разных группировок. Книга издана в 2015 году и получила

в Лондоне на Международном литературном фестивале главный приз – Золотую медаль «Голубь мира».

За пять лет нашего творческого сотрудничества в московском издательстве «Перо» увидели свет повести «Соседушки», «Фарход из Навгилема», семейная книга «Поделись любовью», научные исследования о переводах В. А. Жуковского «К Востоку обращён мой взор» и «Сентиментальное путешествие» – о взаимовлиянии русской и таджикской литературы 20–30-х годов, роман «Свет мой, Солнышко» и книга для детей «Сказки бабушки Гульсифат». А совсем недавно вышли из печати избранные произведения «В этом райском уголке земли...» и публицистический сборник «Настоящий рай – потерянный рай», который я и представляю читателям.

В отдельном разделе этого сборника Гульсифат собрала статьи, написанные в постперестроечные годы. Автора до сих пор волнуют вопросы сохранения лучших национальных традиций и чистоты родного языка («Великие мужи таджиков», «Неважно откуда ты, важно кто ты»).

Рассуждениями о ностальгии и вытекающих из неё последствий полны статьи «Настоящий рай – потерянный рай», «Времён контрасты», «Как чудно жить. Как плохо мы живём...» Гульсифат подтверждает свои мысли цитатами из произведений классиков Джалалиддина Руми, Марселя Пруста, Фридриха Ницше, Бориса Слуцкого, Марины Цветаевой.

Путевые зарисовки написаны Гулей по следам презентаций её книг в разных странах мира. Оказалось, герои Шахиди близки людям независимо от мест их проживания, возраста, национальности. И это открытие стало для автора самым сильным нравственным потрясением в Нью-Йорке и Вашингтоне («Такая близкая и далёкая Америка»), в Тель-Авиве и Иерусалиме («Размышления у Храма Гроба Господня»), в Лериче, Пизе, Флоренции («Италия: Бухта поэтов и новый центр высокого искусства»), в провинциальном городке Суворове Тульской области – невдалеке от родового имения Мишенское гения перевода В. А. Жуковского («Новая встреча на родине В. А. Жуковского»).

Гульсифат Шахиди – член Союза писателей России и член исполнительного и консультативного совета Евразийской творческой гильдии. В Лондоне она познакомилась со многими интересными писателями и поэтами, пишущими на русском языке. Гуля считает полезным и познавательным для себя близко к сердцу принимать творчество современников. Это учёба, позволяющая душе трудиться. Её завораживают образы и идеи Диляры Линдсей (статья «Я научилась звукам доверять...»). А отзыв на книгу казахской писательницы Р. Буркитбаевой-Нукеновой «Завитки каракуля» Гульсифат поэтически назвала «Кувшин женских мелодий Раушан».

В книге другой писательницы Зауре Турехановой «Амина Туран в стране номадов» автор рецензии увидела перекличку с любимой с детства «Алисой в стране

чудес» и восхищается красотой мифологического эпоса и казахского фольклора.

Тронули сердце Гульсифат стихи дагестанского поэта Абу-Суфьяна в сборнике «Журавушка» и для них нашла она особые слова.

Мы были вместе с Гулей в Москве на презентации книги юной писательницы из Южной Африки Меган Вернер «Это зависит от меня, или Семь способов изменить жизнь к лучшему». Меган - подросток поразила нас своим видением жизни и очень благодарила старшую подругу Гульсифат Шахиди за рецензию «Браво, Меган! Или мудрость измеряется не годами».

Хочется особо выделить рецензии Гули на книги наших друзей-земляков, которые мы обсуждали после каждого прочтения. «Всё, кина не будет!» - записки на полях книги Мухиддина Махмудова «Кино Бако Садыкова» - с болью написанные строки. Для нас обеих почитательниц элитного таджикского кино - это непреходящая грусть об его утрате. Мы хорошо знали таджикского Тарковского - творца поэтического кино Бако Садыкова, чьи фильмы получали престижные призы на международных фестивалях. А ныне мастер в забвении живёт в Узбекистане и его уникальные киноленты не сохранились ни в одном кинофонде. Автор книги о Бако Мухиддин Махмудов - верный друг режиссёра собрал под одной обложкой уникальные документы, переписку с Госкино, личные письма, фотографии, киносценарии. И Гуля рецензирует это издание с близкими ей и автору принципами суфизма и бессмертной восточной поэзии.

Книга коллеги-журналиста и земляка Умеда Бабаханова называется «Таджики идут». Гуля в рецензии оставила то же название, написав автору слова благодарности и восхищения его честностью и мужеством как военного корреспондента.

Не остался без внимания моей подруги и нашумевший в Москве роман нашего друга и земляка Владимира Медведева под названием «Заххок». Медведев вырос в Таджикистане, хорошо знает язык, культуру, литературу древнего народа. В гражданскую войну 90-х он встречался с воюющими из разных группировок, брал интервью у командиров бандформирований. А страшный Заххок – это симбиоз человека и рептилии из поэмы Фирдоуси «Шахнаме». Рецензию на роман Гуля назвала «Лишь бы не было войны». Заветное желание всех женщин-матерей жить в мире, не допустить в родных местах кровопролития. С этим желанием и пишет свои книги Гульсифат Шахиди.

В публицистическом сборнике при всём разнообразии жанров есть искорка веселья – зарисовка с натуры юмореска «Процедурный кабинет». Вы уже прошли диспансеризацию, дорогие читатели? Если нет, то два старичка-пенсионера вас научат как правильно её пройти. Читайте и посмеёмся вместе.

Вера Двойниченко,
журналист

СТАТЬИ

ВЕЛИКИЕ МУЖИ ТАДЖИКОВ

С древних времен у таджиков бытует обычай: когда рождается ребёнок, ему под голову кладут рукописный томик мудрости веков – оригинальный текст Корана или книгу газелей Хафиза, который пересказал Коран в стихах. Считается, что это помогает ребёнку вырасти мудрым в жизни и вдохновенным в творчестве.

Такая вера в силу письменного источника не случайна. Именно на Востоке родилось столько величайших учёных и поэтов, талантливых художников и зодчих. Духовное величие народа – это учёные Авиценна, Аль-Хорезми, Аль-Фараби и Аль-Бируни, звёзды первой величины на поэтическом небосклоне Рудаки, Фирдоуси, Хайям, Руми, Саади, Хафиз, Джами. Мастера художественного творчества Борбад, Мани, Бехзод известны далеко за пределами древнего Согда, государства Саманидов и Мавераннахра (Двуречья) – основной территории современной Центральной Азии. Можно спорить о деталях биографии каждого из великих, но бесспорно одно – родным языком названных и многих неназванных классиков той эпохи был персидский.

Древняя наука Востока послужила основой для развития многих областей естествознания и философии. Общеизвестны три столпа науки: Аль-Хорезми (IX–X вв.), открывший основополагающие каноны в арифметике и алгебре и оказавший большое влияние на развитие математики в Западной Европе; Аль-Бируни (IX–X вв.) – философ, прокомментировавший Аристотеля и получивший имя Второй Учитель (то есть второй после Аристотеля), и, конечно же, Авиценна, который считал себя учеником и продолжателем дела великих учёных Запада и Востока. Он обобщил и развил опыт греческих, древнеримских, индийских и азиатских учёных в своём всемирно известном «Каноне врачебной науки».

Средневековая Европа познакомилась с этим шедевром медицинской науки ещё в XII веке, как только он был переведён на латинский язык и в течение пяти столетий «Канон» был теоретическим и практическим руководством для её врачей. Острая потребность в «Каноне врачебной науки» послужила причиной того, что он был издан в Венеции ещё в 1483 году и затем неоднократно переиздавался. Художественные и философские труды Авиценны оказали большое влияние на последующее развитие литературы народов Востока и Запада. Мотивы его художественно-философских повестей можно обнаружить даже в «Божественной комедии» Данте, который упоминает его как выдающегося мыслителя.

Омара Хайяма в Европе знают как поэта – мастера четверостиший, весельчака и вольнодумца, в чьих лаконичных стихах сочетаются глубина, отточенность формы и редкостное остроумие с поразительным жизнелюбием. Но не всем известно, что Омар Хайям, прежде всего, выдающийся математик-астроном, автор математического открытия, впоследствии переоткрытого и названного биномом Ньютона, составитель непревзойдённого до нашего времени по точности календаря, мудрый философ-аристотельянец.

Поэтическое слово для восточных мастеров пера было способом не только выражения собственной вдохновенной мысли и концентрации вековой мудрости народа, но и важным средством воспитания людей и влияния на сильных мира сего. Поэтому, например, Рудаки (IX–X вв.) был не только поэтом, основоположником таджикско-персидской литературы, но и воспитателем: его с уважением называли и называют Устод – учитель. Наставниками поэты Востока были не только в творчестве. Если великий поэт, философ, суфий Джалалиддин Руми (XIII в.) воспитал сына – впоследствии основоположника турецкой поэзии Султана Валада, то мудрый и степенный Джами (XV в.) – поэт, философ, филолог, музыковед – стал учителем и наставником основоположника узбекской литературы Алишера Навои.

Гёте чрезвычайно высоко ценил таджикско-персидскую поэзию. По её мотивам он создал книгу стихов «Западно-восточный диван». Книга оказала огромное влияние на европейскую литературу, на формирование её интереса к восточной поэзии и поэтике.Общепризнанно, что таджикско-персидская поэзия, вобравшая в себя и мудрость, и знания – это учебник жизни, в ней каждый может найти для себя что-то очень ценное, заветное. Для этого по определению Пушкина требуется немногое – по-настоящему понять «правду древнего Востока».

НЕ ВАЖНО ОТКУДА ТЫ, ВАЖНО КТО ТЫ

Нет, наверное, другого такого языка на свете, в котором было бы столько наречий, диалектов и говоров. Вот прилетаю из очередной поездки в любимый Душанбе, встречают меня многочисленные друзья и все спрашивают: «Чи хели, читу шумо, нагз-ми, чи хол дори, сози, тинчи, читарои, тузук хаид-ми?» и т. д. и т. п. И всё это означает одно: как ты или как ты себя чувствуешь? Хотя в настоящее время преобладает один диалект, понятный теперь всем. Вы подумаете, что люди стали выражать свои мысли на языке литературном? Нет, в обычной беседе, на улице и в быту молодёжь больше использует упрощённый южный диалект.

Как летний тёплый ветерок разносит лепестки необыкновенных горных цветов по свету, так и многих из нас разбросала по всему миру матушка-земля наша таджикская. Многие в настоящее время живут в разных уголках планеты и объединяются в диаспоры. Но каждый с нетерпением ждёт встречи с родными местами.

Проезжая каждый раз по главному проспекту города, замечаю, как преображается Душанбе. Радует глаз любимая средняя аллея, которая хоть и завешана теперь большим количеством рекламы, но по-прежнему является главным местом встреч друзей и свиданий влюблённых. Здесь мы видим уважаемых аксакалов – устодов и вместе с ними вспоминаем прошлое...

Годы меняют и город, и людей. Особенно я это чувствую на свадьбах моих друзей и родственников. Когда-то при выборе невесты или жениха много вопросов возникало, из какого региона, района, местности, а иногда даже переулка (!) избранники. По поводу другой национальности вообще речи не могло быть (хотя исключения из правил случались). А ещё изучалась родословная до седьмого колена. Чтобы парень с севера страны женился на южанке или наоборот – это было редкостью и не очень приветствовалось родными, близкими и особенно соседями. Смешно, но было именно так.

Сейчас всё изменилось, и хотя по привычке спрашивают, откуда невеста или жених, по сути молодых и старых это уже мало волнует. Как говорил великий Джалалиддин Руми, не важно, что ты с севера, юга, запада или востока, главное, чтобы в сердце у тебя была Любовь к Истине и человеку.

Я счастлива, что у меня много верных и искренних друзей. Они все из разных регионов, городов, стран. Не представляю себе свою жизнь без их участия. Где бы мы ни жили, нас объединяет главное – искренняя любовь к Отчизне, к своей столице – родному Душанбе...

«НАСТОЯЩИЙ РАЙ – ПОТЕРЯННЫЙ РАЙ»

Сладостность и наслаждение местом отдохновения пропорциональны болезненности странствия. Только тогда ты станешь наслаждаться родным городом и близкими своими, когда ты испытал муки изгнания.

Джалалиддин Руми

Задумывались ли вы о том, что всё в жизни повторяется? Пока мы молоды и беспечны, говорим чаще о будущем. А когда становимся зрелыми и появляется первая седина, недуги и испытания накапливаются

с годами, мы оглядываемся назад. И кажется нам, что вот тогда, в прошлом, было всё хорошо.

Ностальгия – особый вид состояния человека, в котором принципиально важно осмысление собственной жизни и судьбы, положения в обществе. Ностальгия приходит постепенно, как бы крадучись, исподволь. Человек, оказавшись перед грузом прожитых лет, вдруг замечает себя в толпе знакомых и незнакомых людей, которые собрались по поводу какого-либо печального события...

Покинув родину, мы часто думаем, что теперь жизнь будет лучше, счастливее. Но, увы! Счастье, мне кажется, не действительность, а только воспоминание.

Очутившись в чужой стране, мы не всегда находим понимание и сострадание. Бывает, сталкиваемся и с враждебностью, и с нетерпимостью. И тогда тоска по родине становится всё более ощутимой.

Толерантность – замечательная тема для различного рода проектов и конференций. Но в повседневной жизни мы, к сожалению, её почти не чувствуем в некоторых бывших братских республиках.

А вот заграницей другой расклад. Как-то перед праздником Рамазан я пошла за покупками в огромный супермаркет «Азда» (это мировая сеть американских супермаркетов). И вижу такую картину: над каждой кассой и продуктовым отделом висит огромный плакат с восточным пейзажем и поздравлением «Ид мубо-рак!». У меня защемило сердце от радости, и улыбка появилась на лице. Так и шла по магазину, провожаемая

приветливыми взглядами покупателей и продавцов.

Помню, к 40-летию душанбинской газеты «Вечёрка» был показан клип на «Песню о Душанбе» Александра Зацепина, профессионально сделанный по заказу главного редактора иранским оператором Мехди Наини. Этот клип поставили на интернет-сайт "YouTube", который за один день, просмотрели более двенадцать тысяч человек. А вот лишь некоторые из комментариев: «Аж ком к горлу подступил»; «Снято с любовью, спасибо!»; «Ich liebe mein Heimatland! Я люблю тебя, мой родной Душанбе»! «Спасибо автору. Скучаю сильно по Родине. Смотрю, и на душе кошки скребут»; «It's very nice! Zinda bosh, ey vatan!»

Возвращаться на родину всегда приятно, даже через клип в Интернете. Тоска слабеет, и светлые воспоминания не покидают тебя.

Камол Худжанди, известный средневековый поэт, покинув родину, написал пронзительные стихи о родных местах в цикле «Гариби». А великий Саади, половину жизни проведший в скитаниях, подарил потомкам прекрасные газели о любви к родным истокам.

Вспомним беспечный народный фольклор. Говорят пословицы, проверенные временем, незыблемы. Вот, например, «Кто старое помянет – тому глаз вон!» Почему? Может быть, ностальгировать, тосковать, грустить – это болезненное состояние? Или всё же без светлой щемящей грусти человек не может жить? А вот что сказано в другой пословице: «Что было, то прошло, а грех пополам».

Мне по душе мнение Марселя Пруста, «апологета» ностальгии, французского поэта и философа: «Настоящий рай – это потерянный рай!» Просто и ёмко.

ВРЕМЁН КОНТРАСТЫ

Иду по родному Душанбе и думаю о величии классиков. Ощущаю восторг от музыки гениального и светлого Моцарта, от творения Микеланджело или неистового Дали, вспоминаю строки из поэзии Фирдоуси и Шекспира, рубаи – четверостишия о жизни и смерти весельчака Хайяма и останавливаю этот миг. В мечтах они мои единомышленники, друзья, наставники.

Проехавший на скорости по рыхлой дороге после ливня шикарный автомобиль вернул меня в реальность – щедро окатил грязной водой и умчался прочь. Будто чьё-то задание выполнил. Контраст поразил: грязь и грёзы. Как отомстить лихачу-водителю? Кулаком вслед погрозить? Глупо. Да Бог с ним! «В великодушии есть столько же эгоизма, сколько и в мести, только этот эгоизм другого качества», – считал Ницше.

Самый людный перекрёсток центра Душанбе – угол проспекта Рудаки и Дома печати знают все горожане и даже гости столицы. Это своего рода бренд. Здесь продают самый ценный продукт питания населения – лепёшки, и теперь это бизнес, потому товар идёт с наценкой.

Как-то я покупала хлеб, а рядом двое неопрятных мальчишек очень дерзко и отборно бранили друг друга на таджикском языке. Остановила их и попросила не загрязнять нашу родную речь. Посоветовала читать книги Хафиза, Рудаки, Пушкина, нашего современника Мирзо Турсун-заде. На вопрос, знаете, кто такой Пушкин, тотчас услышала ответ: «Александр Сергеевич». Я была приятно удивлена, поскольку никак не ожидала такой быстрой реакции от мальчишек, которые показались мне бездомными и голодными.

Я хорошо помню свои детские и юношеские впечатления от встреч с поэтом Мирзо Турсун-заде. Они с моим отцом вечерами гуляли во дворе наших домов по улице Свириденко (теперь улица Бухоро). Так и слышу его удивительные рассказы о таджикско-персидской поэзии. Тембр его голоса был мягким, мелодичным, особенно при чтении гениальной восточной классики.

В начале восьмидесятых годов уже прошлого столетия на Днях советской литературы, приуроченных

к 70-летию народного поэта Таджикистана Мирзо Турсун-заде, я была на открытии его дома-музея. Мне доверили провести первую экскурсию с гостями – прославленными деятелями мировой литературы. Здесь я познакомилась с выдающимся советским писателем Чингизом Айтматовым, который во время беседы с восхищением отметил, что был только что на родине Мирзо Турсун-заде, в селении Каратаг. Его поразило, как стар и млад наизусть читают стихи Рудаки, Фирдоуси, Хайяма, Хафиза, Саади, Руми, Джами, а также современных поэтов. «А ведь среди них были и седовласые старцы без образования, и дети дошкольного возраста», – удивлялся Чингиз Торекулович.

Чистый лист бумаги впитывает в себя всё – историю, трактаты, поэзию и прозу, музыкальное наследие. А вот человек – самое трагическое и счастливое создание – никак не может усвоить опыт исторических коллизий, парадоксальных явлений во взаимоотношениях цивилизаций. Мне посчастливилось присутствовать на встречах и дискуссиях моих наставников – Вохида Асрори, Гоиба Каландарова и Отахона Латифи, прислушиваться к их мнению при обсуждении философских тем.

Американский писатель Джон Апдайк в одной из телепередач назвал советских читателей удивительным народом. Его поражало, что люди читали и в парке на скамейке, и в лифте, и в метро, а вечера поэзии Евтушенко и Ахмадулиной в 60-е годы не вмещали всех желающих.

Мир электроники и Голливуда навязывает нам американский образ жизни, одновременно разрушая что-то очень трепетное в наших душах. Философы размышляют об этом, издают трактаты, обращаясь к опыту истории. Они считают, что культура – это лишь тоненькая яблочная кожура над раскалённым хаосом бытия, а люди на земле продолжают «гибнуть за металл».

...Те мальчики на душанбинском перекрёстке виновато произнесли «мебахши» (извини), а затем уверенно назвали имя гения: «Александр Сергеевич».

Ещё Достоевский подчеркивал в Пушкине «перевоплощение своего духа в дух чужих народов». Почитайте его «Приношение Корану» и почувствуйте высокую мораль художника. Также созвучны здесь и мысли Гёте о Хайяме и Хафизе. Изолированное существование народов и культур сегодня – фикция. Вот почему уже по-новому возвращается родовое сознание человечества, а значит пора мифа.

«Чем больше мы отдаляемся от советской эпохи, тем больше видим, что это не случайное явление в мировой истории», – сказал Чингиз Айтматов в одном из своих интервью.

Ницше, казалось бы, запутавшись в своих рассуждениях о человеке, о Боге, о религиях, вдруг произносит:

Чтоб жизнь как следует прожить,
Ты должен выше жизни быть!
Учись же возвышаться,
И сверху вниз впиряться!

У водителя маршрутного такси я как-то спросила: «Почему вы говорите со мной на «ты»?» Он непринуждённо ответил мне: «А вас что двое?»

Ум наш в смятении не от того, что знание перевернуло мир, а от того, что не может смириться с этим переворотом. Мы психологически не подготовлены к тайне связи времён. Кто-то, чтобы постичь её, торопит будущее, рвётся вперёд. Кто-то обращает свои взоры исключительно в прошлое. Идеалы удобнее проецировать на те, которые хотя бы частично осуществлялись когда-то. В поисках истины человечество не находит ответы. Борис Слуцкий сказал:

Скоро мне или не скоро в мир отправиться иной –
Неоконченные споры не окончатся со мной.
Начаты они задолго, за столетья до меня.
И продлятся очень долго, очень долго без меня...

...Дождь перестал идти, стало свежо и солнечно. Я решила больше не вспоминать о той шикарной машине, которая так лихо проскочила мимо меня, забрызгав грязью.

«КАК ЧУДНО ЖИТЬ.
КАК ПЛОХО МЫ ЖИВЁМ…»

Прилетаю в Москву в самолёте, переполненном гастарбайтерами. Слово-то какое?! При выходе через таможню вижу, как остановили молодого парня, который и слова не мог сказать по-русски. Вроде все документы в порядке. Пришлось мне на время стать переводчиком. Иначе земляку моему долго пришлось бы доказывать, что он – это он. Парень был просто счастлив от неожиданной помощи, а мне было очень грустно за него.

Писатель Виктор Пелевин, размышляя о норме счастья, положенного человеку в жизни, утверждал, что бы не происходило, этого счастья не отнять. Говорить о том, что хорошо и что плохо, можно, если по меньшей мере знаешь, как и для чего сконструирован человек. И какая разница, что является поводом, если вырабатываемое душами счастье одинаково?

Рано или поздно каждый человек задумывается о смысле своего существования. Многим не решить этот сложный вопрос. Слава Богу, есть такие, кто строит храм в своей душе. Для них главным в жизни является понимание тезиса – я провожу тебя, меня проводят другие.

Время – это пространство между поступком и результатом. Как оно быстротечно, знает каждый, чья жизнь богата действием и поступками. Полный самолёт молодых людей, которые в поисках хлеба насущного отправляются в неизвестность, эта картина остаётся в памяти надолго. Тот парень, который и на родном-то языке говорил на непонятном диалекте и не мог долго объяснить, где значится его фамилия в паспорте, а где имя, в поисках счастья поменял своё тихое родное горное село на жестокий и непредсказуемый мегаполис. Так кем и для чего создан человек? И вновь вопрос Хайяма приходит на память: «Кто и откуда мы?»

На вопрос, куда тебя понесло без профессии, мой попутчик грустно ответил, что нужда погнала в дальние края. Отца убили, а их у матери осталось десять детей. Старший брат два года назад уехал в Россию на заработки и исчез. Дома работы нет, а если и есть, то денег платят мало. «Вся надежда на меня», – закончил он свой грустный рассказ.

Позже мне довелось в Лондоне стать участницей конференции по развитию самосознания и самообразования. Говоря об истинном назначении человека и человечества, руководитель Академии Шейх Фазлулла отметил в своём докладе, что только человек, знающий не понаслышке, что такое страдания, лишения и болезни, может понять другого, ищущего исцеления и поддержки.

Люди – это единый организм, который связан между собой крепкими узами. Не сочувствуя другим, ты в первую очередь не сочувствуешь самому себе. Ведь глобальный мир начинается с личного мира. В конференции приняли участие учёные из разных стран мира, которых объединило желание сказать о недостижимости гармонии, о стремлении понять ближнего – себе подобного.

Всё культурное и эстетическое наследие человечества веками учит нас добродетели – истинной красоты человеческой. Бесценны уроки, которые дают нам книги, картины, шедевры музыкального искусства. Мудрость и не должна быть сложной, унылой и тяжёлой. И как говорится в древних писаниях, в поисках мудрости первый шаг – это молчание, второй – выслушивание, третий – запоминание, четвёртый – применение, пятый – когда ты можешь поделиться своими знаниями с другими...

Как же там мой мимолётный попутчик, паренёк из далёкого горного села? Прощаясь, я спросила, куда же он направляется. Парень ответил: «На Черкизон, там много наших, помогут, наверное».

Черкизовский рынок в Москве закрыли. Куда он подался? А может быть, нашёл брата и всё-таки устроился где-то в другом месте? ...Дай-то Бог. Как прав был Георгий Адамович в стихотворении «Памяти Цветаевой, сказав:

> Не я виной, как много в мире боли,
> Но ведь и вас я не виню ни в чём.
> Всё – по случайности, всё – поневоле.
> Как чудно жить. Как плохо мы живём...

Пока человек способен к состраданию – он жив. Вокруг нас очень многое остаётся неизменным – озеро, гора, речка, родник, родительский дом, родная сторона... Но что-то исчезает, пока ты живёшь. На самом деле это «что-то» теряешь ты сам, когда необратимо проходишь мимо самого главного...

ЮМОРЕСКА

ПРОЦЕДУРНЫЙ КАБИНЕТ

В Москве, впрочем, как и по всей стране, объявили всеобщую... диспансеризацию. И пожилых людей это тоже касается. Похоже, глядя на нас, правительство и решило продлить пенсионный возраст. Заметьте, там наверху не думают о повышении пенсии и хватает ли её для поддержания здоровья, элементарного выживания.

Ну и ладно. Пошли мы тоже с супругой – два пенсионера по приглашению в поликлинику. Нам выписали стопку бумаг для сдачи анализов.

На другой день спозаранку натощак, не емши и не пимши, мы, держась друг за друга, пошли сдавать анализы.

– Галя, а ты бумаги не забыла? – спохватился я.

– Нет, Толенька.

– А баночки с анализами не перепутала?

– Нет, милый. Хотя в нашем возрасте не больно уж их содержимое отличается.

– Ну, я всё же мужчина, дорогая!

– Это у меня надо спросить, милый! – с улыбкой ответила моя Галя.

Так за разговорами и дошли до поликлиники. У процедурного кабинета толпился народ. Мы встали в очередь. Было шумно. Всех, кто пришёл с баночками, отправляли зачем-то в аптеку. Я стал прислушиваться и понял, придётся и нам с Галей бежать туда. Оказывается, теперь анализы принимают только в специальных пластмассовых аптечных ёмкостях.

Аптека рядом была закрыта, и мы пошли в другую.

– Галя, ничего, это очень полезно – ходить утром натощак пешочком. Будто экзамен сдаём на выживание, – пошутил я.

– Мы-то всё выдержим, а вот будущие старики-пенсионеры– вряд ли, – ответила запыхавшаяся от ходьбы Галя.

Купили мы, что велено, и пошли назад. Нам навстречу бежали другие, и старики, и молодые. Видимо, как и нам, им хотелось поскорее поесть. Как диетологи рекомендуют, кушать надо понемногу, но часто и, главное, вовремя. Но какой завтрак, если всё надо было переместить из одного сосуда в другой! Извините за подробности.

Наконец, мы опять встали в очередь. Как только не реагировали люди на всё происходящее. Мало того, что им приходилось стоять дважды, да ещё и от медсестры замечания и укоры выслушивать.

– Почему нас сразу не предупредили об аптечных контейнерах для анализов? – возмущался один.

– Объявления написали, да на дверь повесили бы! – добавил второй.

Медсестра была очень раздражена и боялась, что не успеет всех обслужить до отъезда сборочной машины.

– Чего только не используете вы для анализов! И алюминиевые банки от кофе, и стеклянные ёмкости от мёда, джема и непонятно чего ещё, – бухтела она.

Я не выдержал и шутя зарифмовал:

– Но это же красиво! Лучше же, чем в бутылке от молока или пива.

– Ещё чего! – отрезала медсестра. – Только что один пациент мочу свою в бутылке из-под коньяка принёс! Лаборанткам-то каково?! Времени не остаётся на основную работу!

Тут один из очереди не выдержал и ответил:

– Взяли бы да выпили. Говорят, урина полезнее, чем алкоголь.

В очереди все засмеялись. А у медсестры глаза чуть из орбит не вылезли. Но потом она, не выдержав, тоже засмеялась.

Подошла наша очередь.

– Где ваши направления? – спросила медсестра.

Мы показали свои бумаги. Она посмотрела на нас и спокойно сказала:

– А вам эти анализы сдавать не нужно. Только кровь и флюорография.

Я посмотрел на свою Галю, а она в изумлении взглянула на меня и вздохнула:

– Да, старость – не радость. И столько зря бегали!

– Ничего, Галенька, зато аппетит нагуляли! Пойдём позавтракаем, родная?

ГАЛЕРЕЯ ПОРТРЕТОВ

ГЕННАДИЙ РАТУШЕНКО:
«Фото – зрительная память истории»

Геннадий Ратушенко родился 5 мая 1941 года. Окончил Омский сельскохозяйственный институт по профессии инженер-геодезист. По направлению приехал в 1968 году в Таджикистан, занимаясь аэрофотосъёмкой, неожиданно для себя почувствовал вкус к фототворчеству. 10 лет он был фоторепортёром «Вечернего Душанбе», 20 лет – собственным фотокорреспондентом АПН и РИА «Новости», с 1991 года – председателем Союза фотохудожников Таджикистана. Автор и составитель шести выставок, девяти фотоальбомов, различных эмблем и знаков. Награждён орденом «Дусти».

– Геннадий Петрович, Ваше творчество хорошо известно в республике. А с чего всё начиналось?

– Признаться, в институте по предмету «Фотография» у меня была слабенькая троечка. А вот геодезическая практика на Севере, за Полярным кругом и в Тюменской тайге приворожила своей первозданной красотой и заставила меня заняться фотоделом всерьёз и надолго. Купил советскую лейку «Зоркий-С», просматривал журналы «Советское фото», подружился с телеоператором и фотолюбителем Лёшей Сушенцовым из редакции «Омских теленовостей».

Из своих студенческих лыжных походов по Горному Алтаю к Белухе, по туристским и альпинистским

тропам Кавказа я привозил фоторепортажи в «Омскую правду» и «ТВ-Новости». Конечно, из вороха отснятой плёнки помогал мне отбирать темы Лёша Сушенцов. Кстати, его телесюжеты шли от фотографии. Лаконичные и очень понятные, красивые и точные.

Через два года увлечение фотографией дало плоды – серия моих лирических фото «Восхождение», «Великое таинство» и «Любовь – кольцо...» получила первый приз на областном фотоконкурсе газеты «Омская правда».

– *Кем ощущаете себя больше фотографом или фотохудожником?*

– Для меня всегда было важно художественное творчество. Банально говорить про «третий глаз», но через объектив я научился видеть в жизни необычное в обычном. Внештатно сотрудничая с газетами и телевидением, я получал гонорары, и фотография стала моим вторым ремеслом, но ремеслом творческим.

– *С удовольствием смотрю на старые пожелтевшие фотографии. Мне кажется, в них больше искренности, чистоты.*

– В 60–80-е годы случилось массовое увлечение фотографией. Именно чёрно-белое фото с большей достоверностью передаёт реальность жизни, не отвлекаясь на цветовые пятна. Цвет – приоритет для цветной фотографии. В период дефицита киноплёнки на ТВ в новостных сюжетах и промышленных передачах часто использовалась чёрно-белая фотография. С 1968 года я сотрудничал с душанбинскими телерепортёрами

Михаилом Никулиным, Геннадием Щербатовым, печатался в республиканских газетах «Комсомолец Таджикистана», «Коммунист Таджикистана» и в моей родной «Вечёрке».

В 1980 году я подготовил выставку из ста фотографий по просьбе итальянской стороны «Таджикистан – юг Италии: на одной параллели» и был участником Дней культуры в этой интересной стране. Фотовыставка сохранилась до сегодняшних дней и была бы интересной и для нашего зрителя. Сегодня я непременно включаю в свои цветные фотовыставки и фотоальбомы чёрно-белую фотографию прошлых лет, от которой идёт положительная аура.

– Жизнь быстротечна, и каждый из нас старается запечатлеть мгновения. И часто любительские фото эффектны и эмоциональны, не так ли?

– Согласен, сегодня уже почти каждый десятый – фотолюбитель. У многих есть мобильник с встроенной цифровой камерой, цифровая «мыльница» и почти профессиональная камера, да не одна. В столице растёт армия необученных фотолюбителей! Ведь фотографических ПТУ и фотокружков нет. Даже не на всех факультетах журналистики обучают фотожурналистике. Хотя бытует обывательское мнение, что фотоаппарат сам снимает, щёлкай себе, да щёлкай. Чему тут учиться?

Технология построения изображения одна и та же – через объектив на плёнку или на цифровую матрицу. Цифровая обработка и печать имеет больше творческих возможностей, чем аналоговая, поэтому и прогрессирует. Но я всю жизнь учусь и на собственных ошибках, и на творчестве коллег.

– Мир заполнили глянцевые фото! Иногда шикарно изданные журналы раздаются бесплатно. Что Вы думаете о новой технологии фотоизображения?

Глянцевые журналы я перелистываю равнодушно. Красиво, броско, но бездушно. Меня заботит другое. Более 80 галерей распахнули свои двери во время проведения месячника фотографии в Вене, участником которого мне посчастливилось побывать в ноябре 2006 года. Сто лучших фотографов летом 2006 года были приглашены на съёмку Синьдзянского автономного округа Китая. Есть Дом фотографии в Ташкенте, многочисленные фотогалереи в Москве.

Вот только в Душанбе нет официальной фотогалереи. Кстати, в экспозициях фотогалерей я не встречал глянцевых фотографий. Разнообразные жанры, необычные темы и сюжеты составляют основу выставок. А в нашей республиканской прессе, к сожалению, не на чем остановить взгляд. Заказные, глянцевые выставки, подготовкой которых руководит Минкультуры, не отличаются оригинальностью, продуманной идеологией и художественностью. «Что вижу, то и пою» – смысл этих выставок, но не осмысливание каждого сюжета и образа Таджикистана в целом.

– У каждого из нас в течение жизни набирается много фотоальбомов, кипы фотографий. Как быть с ними? Ведь порой бывает очень трудно расставать-

ся с воспоминаниями о прошлом.

– Надо пожалеть человека, которому вы показываете семейные фотографии. Отберите только важные и интересные, отсканируйте, запишите на CD-диски и храните для потомков, истории. Сделайте цифровые или аналоговые фотоальбомы по темам. А лучше всего доверить ваш архив профессиональному дизайнеру, который с вашей подсказкой может решить эту проблему.

Вообще-то хорошие семейные фотографии в красивых рамочках разных размеров замечательно смотрятся на стенах квартиры, они создают уют и несут положительную ауру и энергетический заряд от ваших предков и вашей юности. Всмотритесь в телеэкран – в любом доме, офисе, на стенах много картин, фотографий. А у вас всё ещё голые стены?

– Геннадий Петрович, кого Вы больше любите снимать – детей или взрослых? А может, деятелей науки и культуры, политиков?

– Я профессиональный фотограф и должен уметь снимать в разных жанрах фотожурналистики и фотоискусства. Любой человек остаётся человеком, в каком бы ранге он не был. А найти его художественный образ всегда сложно. У меня есть несколько фотоальбомов детей разных возрастов – от рождения ребёнка до снятых на заказ. Двадцать лет работы собственным фотокорреспондентом по Таджикистану от АПН и РИА «НОВОСТИ», на журналы и прессу, выходящие в зарубежных странах, – это великолепная журналистская школа!

По количеству и качеству публикаций о Таджикистане за рубежом я входил в первую пятёрку фотокорров РВКС (Редакция внутрисоюзной корреспондентской сети) и мог бы попасть в таджикскую Книгу рекордов Гиннесса, если бы таковая была. По моим фотографиям знали, что такое страна Таджикистан, где 93 % горы, о гостеприимном народе, празднике Навруз и таджикской свадьбе. Из многочисленных поездок по республике в поисках интересных фототем я собрал большую цветную и чёрно-белую фототеку. К сожалению, в результате развала СССР внутрисоюзная корреспондентская сеть перестала существовать. Многие фотографы уехали из Таджикистана. Я же решил сохранить уникальную фототеку и не напрасно – ведь пришлось снимать и создавать новую историю Таджикистана.

– *Говорят, что Вы личный фотограф нашего президента?*

– Президент Эмомали Рахмон приглашал меня в свои поездки на крупнейшие стройки республики и открытие новых объектов. Мне было всегда интересно снимать большого и сильного человека в общении с народом и в кругу семьи. Зачастую он сам организовывал сценки и групповые фото, и мы работали как соавторы фотографии. На Международном Азиатско-Тихоокеанском фотоконкурсе «Жизнь в гармонии» наша фотография «Президент и фотограф» завоевала приз «Фуджи-фильма» в Токио в 2000 году.

В годы становления Республики Таджикистан я сделал фотомонтажную выставку «Трудные дороги сози-

дания», где главное – образ президента. У меня много тематических фотоальбомов – отчётов по поездкам. Был дизайнером и составителем фотокниги «Таджикистан – 10 лет независимости», составил и подготовил дизайн пяти авторских политических фотоплакатов – календарей инаугурации президента на 2007–2008 годы, которые напечатали большим тиражом для жителей Таджикистана. Это один из примеров использования политической фотографии в жизни общества. Сложился уникальный тандем президента и фотографа. Для меня это очень значимо.

– Ваш принцип работы – импровизация или определённый сценарий по постановочному плану?

– Всё течёт, всё меняется. Порой не знаешь, что будет завтра. Будь у меня большое наследство, я смог бы планировать необычные фототемы, экспериментировать с цифровой фотографией, создавать фотокартины, проекты будущих фотоальбомов, построил бы или купил замечательную фотомастерскую, оснащённую дорогим оборудованием. В реальной жизни не получается запланировать всё заранее.

На каком-то промежутке тебя могут обмануть и не выполнить договорные обязательства. Все эти жизненные этапы я проходил. Меня больше всего возмущает необязательность чиновников, давших слово, обещание и не выполнивших их. Я придерживаюсь жизненного правила – иди и работай. Всё равно что-нибудь получится. Экспромтом.

– Среди изданных фотоальбомов есть ли такие,

которыми Вы особенно дорожите? Любимый снимок?

– Я скажу, сколько не издано. Самый интересный фотоальбом «Истаравшан – город на Шёлковом пути», который я практически подготовил к 2500-летнему юбилею города в прошлом Ура-Тюбе. Интересная история, археология, восточный базар, ремесленники, памятники культуры создают неповторимый образ этого древнего города в фотографиях. Один из известных московских фотографов как-то сказал: «Да здесь снимать нечего!» А я снимал Истаравшан 20 лет. На проведение торжеств деньги нашли, а на уникальное издание, увы, не хватило.

Думаю, ещё не поздно издать такой фотоальбом, посвященный 2700-летию Куляба: «Город на перекрёстке эпох» через историю, археологию и реальное возрождение города и окрестностей.

А о севере Таджикистана сделать бы альбом «Древний Ходжент на Сырдарье». Согд, наскальные рисунки Ашта, придорожные автографы, туристические тропы и жемчужины Фанских гор, Пенджикент. Весь этот бесценный фотографический невостребованный ещё материал лежит у меня под слоем пыли. Или «Таджикистан – 93 % горы». Уникальный фотоматериал плюс умение его составить равно замечательному фотопроизведению, которое нужно выпустить в свет большим тиражом. Ведь на земном шаре насчитывается более двадцати миллионов таджиков.

Мне нравится мой первый авторский фотопроспект

«Таджикистан – край у подножия Солнца». Дорог и авторский фотоальбом с логичным журналистским прочтением «Вода – это жизнь». Фотоальбом посвящён Душанбинскому международному форуму пресной воды и стал подарком для участников этого форума. Открывается альбом прошедшей конкурсный отбор моей авторской эмблемой этого форума, что очень значимо для фотохудожника. В соавторстве с мэром города Махмадсаидом Убайдуллоевым я составил большой юбилейный фотоальбом «Душанбе – город мира», где размещено пятьсот фото. Этот альбом был напечатан профессиональной издательской фирмой «Мега Басым» в Турции.

Любимый снимок? Фотографии – это мои дети, которых я люблю. Нелюбимых детей не бывает. Я заряжаюсь положительной энергией от своих первых чёрно-белых фотографий, от семейных снимков, пусть даже любительских. Это же зрительная память истории, а историю надо уважать, ибо она наша жизнь и наше продолжение.

– Я знаю, что Ваш сын тоже занимается фотографией. Что скажите о его работах и будет ли он продолжателем Вашего великолепного мастерства?

– Мой сын Жюльен – студент факультета журналистики РТСУ. Естественно, он занимается фотосъёмкой и компьютерной графикой. Он лучше меня чувствует цвет фотографии, и вся техническая часть лежит на нём. Сын приводит в порядок мою большую цифровую фототеку. Творчество – это высокая планка, до которой нужно дорасти. Жюльену удалось снять улыбку вечно серьёзного ректора РТСУ и быть одним из авторов фотовыставки «Новые имена в фотографии».

– *Есть ли у Вас фотостудия?*

– Больной вопрос о фотостудии. В 1996 году мой коллега выкупил по своим каналам в личную собственность двухэтажное помещение АПН – РИА «Новости» на проспекте Рудаки, 18. Здесь на первом этаже размещалась моя фототека, единственная в республике цветная проявочная лаборатория и Союз фотохудожников Таджикистана, который мы зарегистрировали в Минюсте в 1991 году. Помню дождливый день Навруза 1996 года, когда теперь уже новый хозяин предложил демонтировать фотолабораторию, фототеку и освободить ставшие мне родными стены. Этот нокаут, жёсткий удар перестройки я не могу забыть и не оправился от него до сих пор. Какая польза от людей, которые приватизируют блага для собственной наживы, ничего не отдавая государству?

Моя двухкомнатная квартира стала хранилищем фототеки – ценнейшего достояния, истории Таджикистана и местом для компьютера. Четвёртый год власти не дают мне разрешения на постройку мансарды над своей квартирой для использования под мастерскую. В Астане на пятиэтажной хрущёвке настраивают по этажу и сверху ещё красивые мансарды, расширяя площади под жильё. Кстати, мой авторский проект фотогалереи «Душанбинский Арбат» в сквере имени 800-летия

Москвы был опубликован в «Вечёрке» 22 февраля 2007 года как предложение по улучшению облика столицы.

Этот проект был одобрен мэром города и архитекторами на заседании Горсовета. Но вместо величественной стеклянной, прозрачной для осмотра фотографий галереи фирма ООО «Империя Восток» как бы в насмешку сделала на стене у Театра оперы и балета несколько застеклённых рамок. Для кого и для чего? Так и стоит одинокий любимый нами малопосещаемый величественный центр культуры среди шашлычного дыма, ресторанов и питейных заведений. А народ хочет зрелища! Народ хочет иметь профессиональную студию, где можно было бы заказать фотопортрет у профессионального фотохудожника, где можно было бы приобрести замечательную фотографию для дома, для семьи, для офиса и дачи. Где можно было бы получить консультацию по фотоделу, научиться азам фотографии.

– Сейчас в городе много рекламных щитов, порой безвкусных именно в художественном решении. Не обращались ли к Вам с предложением украсить город рекламной продукцией?

– Заказчики рекламной продукции, наверное, забывают, что существует творческий Союз фотохудожников, который может подготовить и выполнить заказ на любую профессиональную рекламу с авторской фотографией. Город «украшают» щиты с пришлой, не таджикской фотографией. Наверное, заказчик не патриот своей Родины.

Жизнь подсказывает, что творческим союзам пришло время объединяться. Поэтому мы провели эксперимент. На базе большого помещения Союза архитекторов объединились под одной крышей Союз фотохудожников и турецкая издательско-полиграфическая фирма «Мега Басым». Общими усилиями мы подремонтировали внутреннюю часть здания и 5 мая 2007 года открыли отчётную юбилейную фотовыставку в честь 65-летия Геннадия Ратушенко и 40-летия фоторепортёрства в Таджикистане. Было бы логично найти способ закрепить юридически этот Дом архитекторов под наш тройственный союз, который мог стать творческим центром профессионалов по интересам. Надеюсь, надеюсь...

В столице бурно развивается строительная индустрия разного назначения. Дорогие стены остаются «голыми» или их украшают стандартными постерами или низкопробными массовыми фотографиями и восточной штампованной дешёвкой. Поэтому архитекторам нужно работать в союзе с фотохудожниками, проектируя заранее места для офисной фотографии в замкнутом пространстве и размещении художественной фотографии для интерьеров. Поэтому сейчас мы создаём большую фототеку из интересных авторских фотографий в надежде, что она будет востребована.

– Позвольте поблагодарить Вас за очень интересную и содержательную беседу и пожелать Вам – первому фоторепортёру «Вечернего Душанбе» успехов и исполнения всего задуманного.

МУРИВАТ БЕКНАЗАРОВ:
«Я – горец, и этим всё сказано»

Беседа с известным художником, заслуженным деятелем искусств Таджикистана – Муриватом Бекназаровым.

– Ваше имя Муриват – от слова «мурувват», переводится как мужественный, благородный, любезный, добрый, благочестивый. Родители видно вложили в него самое сокровенное? Расскажите, пожалуйста, о своём детстве, семье, первых шагах в искусстве живописи.

– В нашей семье у родителей было четверо детей, а я – третий ребёнок. Когда мне исполнилось три года, семья лишилась отца. Маме пришлось одной воспитывать нас. Сколько же сил и мужества надо было иметь, чтобы в те военные, трудные годы прокормить малышню! Наверное, мама поэтому так рано ушла из жизни. Светлая ей память!

С детства я любил рисовать. В те годы в школах помимо общеобразовательных предметов дети могли заниматься в различных кружках. Я выбрал изобразительное искусство – из того изокружка берёт начало моё творчество.

– Ваше детство прошло в горах Памира. Это, конечно же, не могло не повлиять на Вас как на будущего живописца и монументалиста. Какие образы,

мотивы и цвета изобилуют в Вашем творчестве?

– Я думаю, что первые впечатления от окружающего мира остаются с человеком на всю его жизнь, а природа для художника становится частью его самого. С годами эти впечатления могут проявляться самым неожиданным образом и в мировосприятии, и в творчестве. Например, увидев какое-нибудь величественное архитектурное сооружение в Европе или потрясающую скульптуру в Индии, я ловил себя на том, что сравнивал их с величественными горами своего детства.

Кажется, что и художником-монументалистом я стал благодаря интуитивной тяге ко всему объёмному, великому. Но вместе с тем для меня чем разнообразнее образы и мотивы, тем интереснее их воплощение, а цветовое решение картины каждый раз зависит от конкретной задачи.

– Вы работаете в разных жанрах, занимаетесь техникой мозаики и настенной росписью. А живопись выделяете?

– В советское время уделялось больше внимания развитию монументального искусства. Я выполнил немало работ в технике мозаики и настенной росписи в Таджикистане и других союзных республиках. Но с распадом СССР монументальное искусство постепенно перестало существовать. А станковой живописью я занимался всегда. В живописи меня привлекает возможность подняться над обыденностью. Я – горец, и этим всё сказано!

– Ваши работы выставлены в музеях и част-

ных коллекциях Франции, Италии, Германии, Швеции, России, США. А как часто Вы показываете своё творчество в Душанбе?

– В Душанбе проводились две мои персональные выставки – в 1989 году в музее им. Бехзода и в 2002 году в культурном центре «Бактрия». Опять оглянусь на прошлое. В советское время жизнь художников была чрезвычайно насыщенной: проводились ежегодные республиканские и всесоюзные выставки, во всем чувствовалась поддержка государства. Яркий пример тому – стипендия Союза художников СССР, которая присуждалась молодым перспективным художникам из разных республик. Благодаря этой стипендии живописцы в течение двух лет могли заниматься только творчеством. По окончании срока в Москве устраивалась отчётная выставка стипендиатов. Мне тоже повезло в конце 70-х получить такую стипендию, и это послужило стимулом для творчества. К сожалению, нынешние молодые художники лишены такой поддержки.

– Вы учились в Душанбе, а затем в Таллине. Расскажите о своих учителях. Есть ли среди Ваших учеников те, чьи работы особенно цените?

– Учился я в Республиканском художественном училище (1958–1963 гг.) в мастерской прекрасных художников А. Бесперстова и Д. Сафоева. Продолжил учебу в Таллине в Эстонском государственном художественном институте на отделении монументального искусства. Я попал в мастерскую профессора Валериана Лойка, талантливого и обаятельного человека, который 20 лет учился у лучших мастеров Парижа. После окончания университета я 15 лет преподавал в Душанбе в Республиканском художественном училище им. Олимова, затем девять лет в Таджикском техническом университете. Многие из моих бывших студентов – ныне успешно работающие художники. Среди них Азамат Атаханов (Москва), Ринат Анимаев (Париж), Манучехр Сабиров (США), Бахриддин Сангинов (Ходжент), Бахтиёр Одинаев (Душанбе).

– Каков источник Вашего вдохновения?

– Источником и импульсом для вдохновения могут быть самые разные вещи: созерцание горных ущелий, беседа с мудрым человеком, прекрасный женский облик, хорошая живопись или классическая музыка всех времен.

– Что значит для Вас расхожая фраза «художник должен быть свободен»?

– Большие художники и в условиях полной несвободы творили прекрасные вещи, ибо внутренне они были свободны. Для художника во все времена и в любых ситуациях важнее внешней свободы от чего бы то ни было ценилась внутренняя связь с миром, полнокровная жизнь с постоянным обменом энергий в соприкосновении с природой, людьми, искусством.

– Вы служили в рядах Советской армии. Какое у Вас звание и осталось ли в памяти какое-нибудь интересное воспоминание о военной службе? И что пожелаете сегодняшним солдатам и военнослужащим?

– Служил я в Ташкенте, был рядовым, работал художником- оформителем в военной части. Самое большое впечатление произвели на меня командир и замполит нашей части – таких умных и эрудированных военных я редко встречал. А какая была у нас библиотека! Кстати, моими стараниями наша часть была самой профессиональной и красочно оформленной во всей дивизии. Сегодняшним солдатам и военнослужащим пожелал бы образованности, чтобы они любили Родину и служили ей верно.

– *Какое событие в Вашей жизни стало незабываемым?*

– Моя поездка в Индию и Непал в 1990 году. Я соприкоснулся с древней культурой этих сказочных стран. Особое впечатление на меня произвели тысячелетняя скульптура и настенная живопись. Я очень люблю античное искусство, великие творения греческих и римских скульпторов и зодчих, но то, что я увидел в Индии и Непале, не передать словами.

– Вы художник, ваша супруга Лола Толис – композитор. Говорят, двум творческим личностям в одном доме ужиться очень сложно. Это действительно так?

– У нас есть понимание в главном: в отношении к жизни и искусству, а также интерес к творчеству друг друга. А остальные разногласия по мелочам не существенны и преодолимы.

«Я много ездил по миру, знал много художников, но подлинных среди них единицы. Именно к таким относится Муриват Бекназаров».

Пьер-Доминик Поннель,
немецкий дирижёр

ПРЕЛЮДИЯ НАВРУЗА

Есть люди, с которыми всегда чувствуешь себя непринуждённо: с ними легко общаться, душа у них как на ладони. Более сорока лет я близко знакома с Зарриной Миршакар – прекрасной женщиной, талантливым композитором. Но каждая встреча с ней – это неповторимые моменты, душевность и искренность общения.

Навруз для неё всегда двойной праздник – и Новый год по восточному календарю, и день рождения. И именно в Навруз Заррина Мирсаидовна в свой юбилей любезно согласилась ответить на мои вопросы.

– Говорят, что талант – это синтез вдохновения, данного свыше и опыта, приобретённого на земле. Творчески одарённые люди своими произведениями доказывают божественное начало. Интересно, как это происходит?

– На мой взгляд, талант – врождённое качество, и этим всё сказано. Он есть, либо его нет. Когда мы видим потрясающие детские рисунки или слышим великолепную игру ребенка на музыкальном инструменте, мы говорим – какой он одарённый! Здесь не приходится говорить об опыте, который накапливается и приобретается годами. Вдохновение же, как сказал Чайковский, та гостья, которая не любит посещать ленивых. Ты должен ежедневно работать, верить, быть в постоянном поиске и вдохновение явится к тебе. Поэтому, думаю, талант – это и вдохновение, и опыт, и огромное трудолюбие. А синтез всего этого приводит к появлению выдающихся творений.

– Вы из очень известной семьи народного поэта Таджикистана Мирсаида Миршакара. А талант передаётся по наследству? Кстати, вот что прислал Вам пианист Сергей Арзуманов из Нью-Йорка:

> Каждый знает – юн и стар,
>
> Что Заррина Миршакар
>
> В фортепьянных пьесах «Байты»
>
> Рассказала детям байки.
>
> Взяв в наследство от отца,
>
> Мирсаида-мудреца
>
> Дар к лирической струне
>
> И любовь к родной стране!

– Как приятно и неожиданно! Спасибо Сергею за то, что помнит обо мне.

Я счастлива, что родилась в такой творческой семье. Папа Мирсаид Миршакар был не только известным поэтом, но и прекрасно рисовал, любил музыку. Мама моя Гульчехра всегда заражала нас оптимизмом, любила петь и танцевать, благо голос у неё был прекрасный от природы. И ещё она великолепно вязала.

Талант – Божий дар и его необходимо подпитывать в семье, в школе и суметь направить в нужное русло. Нам – детям очень повезло, в семье всегда царила творческая атмосфера. Родители часто водили нас

в театры. Вечерами в нашем доме собирались поэты, композиторы, которые читали новые стихи, играли на фортепиано новые произведения. Куда бы мы летом не выезжали с родителями, мы обязательно посещали концертные залы, театры и музеи. Мой брат Акмал – ныне признанный художник, чьи картины украшают частные коллекции мира. Кстати, все четверо его детей прекрасно рисуют, а дочь Рухмина сочиняет стихи. Моя сестра Зульфия тоже пишет прекрасные стихи и рассказы, брат Афзал – мастер двустиший и отличный рассказчик.

– После окончания Душанбинского музыкального училища Вы продолжили своё образование в Москве в лучшей консерватории мира у выдающихся педагогов. Какие воспоминания Вам особенно дороги?

– Первые встречи с композиторами Юрием Тер-Осиповым, Сергеем Баласаняном, Эдуардом Хагагортяном. Впоследствии они стали моими дорогими учителями, с которыми я общалась до последних дней их жизни.

Кстати, мой отец был членом Комитета по ленинским и государственным премиям. Однажды на одно из заседаний он взял меня с собой – я никогда не забуду этот день в моей жизни. Там я встретилась с Дмитрием Шостаковичем, Арамом Хачатуряном и Николаем Тихоновым. Воспользовавшись моментом, я показала свои прелюдии Дмитрию Дмитриевичу и поразилась его спокойной речи, даже чуть стеснительной. Он робко и деликатно дал мне понять, что надо много работать. Очень жалею, что не сделала тогда фотоснимков.

Представляете, какой был бы у меня архив! Поездки, знакомства с коллегами-музыкантами из ближнего и дальнего зарубежья – всё это тоже незабываемые впечатления. Мои друзья Гульджамиля из Алматы, Катя Коноваленко из Германии, Душан Михалек и Бенжамин Юсупов из Израиля, Радан Вранешевич из Италии всегда поддерживали и поддерживают меня. Перефразируя Хемингуэя, хочу сказать, что такие встречи – это праздник, который останется со мной на всю жизнь.

– А вот сюрприз! Пожелания Ваших друзей из Израиля.

Бенжамин Юсупов, композитор, дирижёр:

«Я считаю Заррину Миршакар одной из самых талантливых таджикских композиторов. Её творчество – это ярчайший пример сочетания глубокого народного начала с высочайшим мастерством и изяществом письма. Она высокообразованный человек и была всегда для меня примером настоящей таджикской женщины».

Душан Михалек, музыковед:

«Для слушателей это было просто потрясающе: твои «Байты» играл молодой пианист из Хорватии Даниел Детони – сын композитора Дубравка. Я объявил публике, что ты посвятила эти пьесы мне. Итак, твоя музыка прозвучала в святом городе Иерусалиме».

– Какое из произведений Вам особенно дорого?

– Я люблю все произведения. Они разные, но в каждом я оставила частичку своей души. Конечно, приятно слышать вот такие отзывы специалистов.

«У Заррины небольшое количество сочинений, но каждое произведение – это весомая страница творчества. Доказательством сказанного служит исполнение «Поэмы-сонаты для кларнета соло», включённой в обязательную программу конкурса кларнетистов в Ленинграде в 80-х годах. Стиль композитора, в отличие от других, выражен диалектом памирской речи. Памирский фольклор и связанные с ним художественные ценности являются основой её музыки и реализуются на уровне языка, драматургии, идейной концепции. Категория национального в произведениях Заррины Миршакар изменчива, она несёт в себе традиции обновления. Перечислю произведения композитора: симфония, симфониетта, симфоническая поэма «Краски солнечного Памира», «Памирские картинки», «Соната-поэма для кларнета соло», «Соната для гобоя соло», «24 байта» для фортепиано, концертино «Респиро» («Дыхание») для скрипки, камерного оркестра и литавр», – отметила в одной из своих статей музыковед, кандидат искусствоведения, доцент Таджикской национальной консерватории Лариса Назарова.

– Как Вы думаете, что такое современная музыка? В наше время мы слышим очень много противоречивых суждений, как, впрочем, и в эпоху деятельности наших отцов.

– Кто-то из поэтов в своё время сказал, что слишком далеко увела композиторов высокая современная техника. И их произведения – это уже нечто превышающее уровень человеческого восприятия. Не всегда и не всеми сразу принималось всё новое в музыке, поэзии, живописи. Понимание приходило постепенно. Требовалось время, чтобы осмыслить, пропустить через себя и принять новаторские формы и идеи и выбирать – использовать это или не использовать в своём творчестве. В своё время «Деревенскую симфонию» Моцарта не приняли, хотя сейчас это произведение признано выдающимся творением. Импрессионисты, модернисты, авангардисты проходили сложный путь признания. Появление нововенской школы Шёнберга, Веберна, Берга воспринято было неоднозначно. Но время показало, что их творения – это новая страница в музыке XX столетия.

Сейчас современные композиторы используют электронную и компьютерную технику. У нас нет возможности на сцене услышать такого рода произведения, поэтому я не могу сказать, нравится мне всё это или нет.

– Говорят, что наша национальная консерватория в республике открылась слишком поздно, но лучше поздно, чем никогда. Можно ли решить проблемы развития современного музыкального искусства только лишь с помощью такого вуза?

– Открытие консерватории – это подарок президента Эмомали Рахмона нам, работникам искусства. Пользуясь моментом, хотела бы от себя лично и от имени всего коллектива выразить благодарность нашему президенту.

Консерватория молодая и, естественно, у нас проблемы – нехватка профессиональных кадров, учебно-методической литературы. К сожалению, очень мало студентов обучается на струнном и духовом отделениях. Это приведёт к тому, что некем будет пополнять оркестр оперного театра. Думаю, это связано с тем, что после окончания республиканской средней специальной музыкальной школы им. Шахиди, школы им. Малики Сабировой, колледжа им. Бобокулова выпускники поступают в другие вузы, а не в консерваторию. Ещё одна проблема – местонахождение специальных музыкальных школ. Школа им. Шахиди готовила и пока ещё готовит выпускников к поступлению в наш вуз. Недавно преподавателями консерватории, деятелями культуры было подписано письмо-обращение к президенту страны о переводе Республиканской специальной музыкальной школы в центр города. Сейчас, слава Богу, письму дали ход. Мы очень надеемся, что найдётся здание (ближе к консерватории), и школа пополнится одарёнными детьми, желающими заниматься музыкой. А лет через десять результаты не заставят себя ждать, было бы желание, стремление, вера.

– На концерте, посвящённом юбилею Шостаковича, прозвучал новый вокальный цикл Заррины Миршакар. Я общалась с музыкантами, которые очень тепло говорили о Вашем творчестве. Хотелось бы привести некоторые отзывы.

Нигина Обидова, доцент Таджикской национальной консерватории:

«Мы с Зарриной знакомы уже много лет. Прежде всего, хочу сказать, что это замечательный человек и прекрасный композитор. Её сочинения для фортепиано и камерных ансамблей – это блестящий синтез эстетики памирских мелодий и мироощущения автора. «Блики» для фортепиано (2003 г.) композитор посвятила мне, и я стала первым исполнителем этих миниатюр. А ещё с огромным удовольствием исполняю её пьесы для фортепиано и ансамбля скрипачей. Кстати, «Три памирские фрески» для скрипки и фортепиано, исполненные на днях нашей скрипачкой Шафак Касымовой в Париже, прошли на ура!»

Оят Сабзалиева, народная артистка Таджикистана, профессор Таджикской национальной консерватории:

«О Заррине можно говорить часами и только хорошее. Мы жили с ней в одной комнате в общежитии Московской государственной консерватории. Помню, в 6 часов утра звучал гимн Советского Союза по радио, а она уже была в репетитории и готовилась к занятиям. С особым волнением и старанием она готовилась к классу (уроку) Сергея Баласаняна. Он буквально «опустошал» её своими требованиями. Был строг и бескомпромиссен.

Однажды у меня был классный вечер – я пела в Малом зале консерватории. Было много друзей и знакомых, и, конечно, Заррина. Потом мы вернулись в общежитие и увидели красиво накрытый стол – это было делом рук моей лучшей подруги Заррины. Сегодня я

хочу пожелать ей доброго здоровья и значительных успехов в творчестве».

В Википедии о моей собеседнице, подруге Заррине Миршакар сказано: «Первая и единственная женщина-композитор Памира», «Первая известная женщина-композитор в Таджикистане».

Добавлю, имя Заррина означает светлая, сильная, золотая, лучезарная, сияющая, как утренняя заря. Сияй и радуй нас, Заррина!

ЖЕНЩИНА
С СИЛЬНЫМ ХАРАКТЕРОМ

Гульчехра Шарипова, кандидат политических наук, Государственный советник юстиции первого класса. Она из числа тех женщин, которых запоминаешь на всю жизнь. Гульчехра образованна, эрудированна, успешна в работе. Всегда приветлива и с ней интересно беседовать. Кроме того, она прекрасная жена и нежная мать. А ещё она пишет стихи.

— Гульчехра, а как Вы относитесь к женскому празднику?

— Я удивляюсь тому, что он однодневный? Наши женщины уже давно заслужили право на внимание и равноправие. Все тяготы лихолетья они перенесли наравне с мужчинами. Кстати, Вы не задавались вопросом, почему в нашем любимом городе Душанбе нет ни одного памятника женщине? Разве не найдётся достойных? А великая поэтесса Зебуннисо? А героиня становления Советской власти в Таджикистане Зайнаббиби? А всемирно известная балерина, славная Малика Сабирова? Да, просто памятник женщине-матери, наконец. Это лишь дань уважения ей...

— Действительно, памятника нет. Я об этом диже не задумывалась. А Каким Вы видите тип деловой женщины современного Таджикистана?

– О-о, у меня очень большие требования к таким женщинам! Деловая женщина в моём понятии – это сначала чиновник, а потом всё другое. Прежде всего, она должна быть компетентна в работе и корректна в общении. В ней должно полностью отсутствовать зазнайство и высокомерие. Всегда смешно выглядят люди и не только женщины, занятые самолюбованием, горделиво поглядывающие на всех с высоты своей значимости, чаще всего мнимой. Гордиться, конечно, можно, но только реальными достижениями, а не временным пребыванием в кресле. Деловая женщина должна отличаться умением одеваться не кривляво-вызывающе, а стильно. А ещё обязательный компонент для неё – интеллект.

– *Легко ли быть в форме на государственной службе?*

– Нелегко. Но это необходимо. Честно говоря, встречают-то всё равно по одёжке. Я добавлю – по внешнему виду.

– *Может ли женщина успевать везде – и на работе, и дома, и при этом выглядеть хорошо?*

– Может, если она очень этого захочет. Всё в её руках.

– *Везде ли Вы успеваете?*

– Мне иногда не хватает 24 часов в сутки.

– *А как же семья?*

– Семья для меня – всё! Я убеждена, что все успехи в карьере зависят от того, какая у тебя атмосфера в семье.

– *Ваши основные направления деятельности?*

– Вопросы международных связей, регистрации нормативных правовых актов министерств, ведомств, общеобязательного характера, институт повышения квалификации работников юстиции и другие.

– Вас знают как женщину с сильным характером. А кто оказал влияние на становление Вашего характера?

– Мой отец Холбобо Шарипов, воспитавший многих известных спортсменов. Он оказал колоссальное влияние на меня. Папа был светлым, благородным, сильным человеком, предельно простым и доступным. Главный его девиз – скромность. Для него все были равны: и высокий чиновник, и простой дехканин. Он никогда не болел звеёдной болезнью. Был весёлым и добродушным, но в то же время прямолинейным и бескомпромиссным человеком, способным безбоязненно и честно высказывать своё мнение, невзирая на последствия, которые не всегда складывались благополучно для него. Физически не выносил интриганство, фальшь и подхалимство. Папа всегда был готов поддержать любого, кто нуждался в его помощи. Люди за это его любили.

– В Вас заложены качества лидера, этому как-то способствовал отец?

– Безусловно. Прежде всего, это глубочайшее доверие ко мне. Он никогда не опускался до мелкой подозрительности, был предельно открыт со мной, видел и уважал во мне человека. Всего один раз в жизни он сказал мне, тогдашней школьнице: «Дочка, не подведи

меня!» Эти слова крепко засели в моей памяти. Папы уже давно нет с нами, а я всё стараюсь его не подвести.

– Женщина на ответственных постах – это закономерность или дань какой-нибудь пропорции?

– Ныне это уже вполне закономерное явление. Известный Указ Президента Республики Таджикистан «О повышении роли женщин в обществе» 1999 года возымел своё действие, теперь женщина на государственной должности – не диковинка.

– Мне кажется, женщина-политик очень редкое явление в нашем современном обществе. А президентом Таджикистана может стать женщина?

– Почему нет? Славная таджикская земля породила немало талантливых сыновей, породит и дочерей. Может, где-то уже и растёт девчушка, способная когда-нибудь возглавить нашу страну. Кстати, как известно, Восток всегда славился мудростью женщин. Ведь недаром именно на Востоке чаще всего пост главы государства или правительства занимали женщины. Вспомним, к примеру, Индиру Ганди в Индии, Сиримаво Бандаранаике в Шри-Ланке, Коросон Акино в Филиппинах, Беназир Бхутто в Пакистане, Тансу Чиллер в Турции. Они по лидерству ни в чём не уступали мужчинам.

– Но почему-то наш менталитет, особенно в сельской местности, не позволяет женщине ставить себя выше мужчины в решении многих житейских вопросов. Знают ли женщины свои права?

– Права правами, но эти знания не должны являться средством конфронтации в семейных взаимоотношениях. Вряд ли так уж нужно разумной женщине ставить себя выше своего мужа, даже если в чём-то он уступает ей. Сила женщины и заключается в том, чтобы наряду со знаниями суметь сохранить мир в доме.

– Вы бы хотели жить при матриархате?

– Нет.

– *Есть ли границы дозволенного для женщин и для мужчин?*

– Скажу так: то, что позволительно мужчинам, непростительно для женщин.

– *Гармония семейных отношений и тепло семейного очага зависят только от женщины?*

– «Погода в доме» зависит от жены. Это моё глубокое убеждение. В домашнем пространстве и ураган, и полный штиль, и лёгкий бриз под мягким солнцем – дело рук жены.

– *Скажите, какие черты характера Вы в себе недолюбливаете?*

– Прямолинейность. Но иначе не могу, будет нечестно. Да ещё доверчивость, пожалуй.

– *Вас часто обманывали?*

– Не часто. Но если это случается, то теряю веру в такого человека навсегда.

– *По роду службы Вы чаще всего работаете с мужчинами. Не чувствуете с их стороны снисхождения?*

– Однозначно не ответишь. В моём понимании служба – это открытое, честное, равноправное партнёрство. Если этого не происходит, работа становится неинтересной.

– Что Вас может неприятно удивить в некоторых мужчинах?

– Наличие женских черт в характере.

– А именно?

– Тяга к сплетням.

– Я заметила, что Вы любите отвечать кратко, тогда блиц-вопросы. Как Вы можете охарактеризовать недруга?

– Это движущая сила, благодаря которой прогрессируешь.

– А скупость?

– Вечное болото, что не попадёт, всё засасывает и всё мало.

– Ревность?

– Наверное, это жадность собственника.

– Глупость?

– Пустота беспредельная.

– Иногда нам – женщинам бывает грустно. Что Вы делаете, когда беспокойно на душе?

– В минуты грусти я слушаю классическую музыку. Особенно произведения Арама Хачатуряна, Равеля, люблю Верди.

– А кто из современных исполнителей Вам нравится?

– Люблю песни Земфиры и Далера Назарова.

– А что бы Вы хотели сказать женской половине в этот праздничный день?

– Желаю всем женщинам ощущать заботу, внимание, бережное отношение, глубокое уважение и искреннюю

любовь своих мужчин не однодневно, а на протяжении всего года. А тем, кто ещё не обзавёлся семьей, желаю обрести уверенность в счастливом будущем. К нему надо стремиться с открытым сердцем и чистыми помыслами.

ПУТЕВЫЕ ЗАРИСОВКИ

ТАКАЯ БЛИЗКАЯ И ДАЛЁКАЯ АМЕРИКА

По жизни я романтик. Люблю путешествовать. Запомнила в детстве слова моей бабушки: «Дидагиату хондагиат мемонад», что в переводе с таджикского означает: «Остаётся лишь то, что увидел и прочёл». Она учила нас – своих внуков не уделять много внимания материальным благам, а тратить их на то, чтобы увидеть мир и читать больше книг. Теперь я понимаю её лучше, чем тогда в детстве. Она была из знаменитого и богатого рода служителей эмирата Благородной Бухары. Бибиджон (бабушка), и это редкость для того времени, росла образованной девочкой. С приходом Ок-

тябрьской революции в один день семья её потеряла всё. Бабушке пришлось работать учительницей в сельской школе и одной воспитывать пятерых детей. А её муж – мой дедушка, известный востоковед, вначале попал в тюрьму за родословную, потом ушёл на фронт и погиб смертью храбрых. Все их дети получили высшее образование. А бабушка любила повторять, что всё в жизни тленно. Нетленна лишь память.

Вот и получается, передала в наследство мне моя бибиджон любовь к книгам и путешествиям. А теперь, к моему удивлению, сама я стала писательницей. Я благодарна, что мои соотечественники во многих уголках земли приглашают меня на презентации и творческие вечера. Езжу с удовольствием, чтобы знакомиться со своими читателями. Спасибо моим трём сыновьям, которые всегда меня в этом поддерживают. А недавно меня пригласили в Нью-Йорк и Вашингтон. Честно признаюсь, сомневалась, смогу ли перенести долгий перелёт. Годы-то уже немолодые.

Организовали поездку мои друзья – Ирена Арзутова, промоутер, продюсер, директор концертной программы «Арз-опера», Давид Гвиниадзе – президент и художественный руководитель фонда «Таланты мира». А в Нью-Йорке меня уже встречали друзья и родственники – племянник Парвиз Шахиди, сын друзей нашей семьи Хусравбек Муродов и главный организатор творческого вечера Наталья Кордо – менеджер программ «Девидзон-радио», вещающем в городе на английском и русском языках. Основная аудитория слушателей –

выходцы из бывшего Советского Союза и, конечно же, республик родной Средней Азии. Наталья Кордо заранее, до моего приезда сделала со мной интервью и всю неделю вместе с рекламным роликом о предстоящей встрече его повторяли на радио «Девидзон».

В Нью-Йорке в небольшом и уютном концертном зале радиоцентра собрались представители многих национальностей, которые говорили на русском языке. Вести вечер мне помогали племянники Парвиз и Джониз, которые недавно обосновались в Бруклине. Большая группа поддержки была из Таджикистана и Узбекистана. Собравшиеся с интересом слушали историю о рождении и выпуске моих книг – повести «Соседушки» (рассказы о судьбах таджикских женщин) и об исследовательской работе о гении перевода В. А. Жуковском «К Востоку устремлён мой взор». Было много вопросов и отзывов.

К моей радости, здесь я встретилась со своей подругой Точинисо Рауповой, с которой мы долгие годы работали в Академии наук Таджикистана. Она специально приехала из другого штата, из города Мэриленда, чтобы увидеться со мной. Кстати, когда Точинисо выступала, один из присутствующих спросил меня: «Это ваша редактор Вера?», на что Точинисо ответила: «Да, я и вера, и надежда, и любовь! Но не Дейниченко». Познакомилась я и с другой Точинисо – родственницей моей подруги. Вот и ходила я меж двух Точинисо всё своё пребывание в Нью-Йорке и загадала много желаний. От души благодарна им за внимание и поддержку. Они мне показали много достопримечательностей го-

рода. Увиделась я и со своими родными Расули из Самарканда, дочерьми моих друзей, милыми девочками Зарнигор и Марджоной.

Гостиница, в которой я остановилась, называлась «Пьерре», она входит в сеть индийских «Тадж-отелей» (наверное, от имени Тадж-Махал) и находится на Манхэттене у Центрального парка города. На следующее утро из-за разницы во времени я проснулась рано. Было очень тепло, и я открыла окно. Каково же было моё удивление, когда на улице услышала таджикскую речь. Узнала, что в парке с раннего утра (чтобы быть первыми в очереди) работают извозчиками на красиво украшенных фаэтонах молодые таджикские парни из Самарканда. Звали их Бехруз, Искандар и Чамшед. Мы побеседовали. Они катали детвору по огромному парку и этим зарабатывали на жизнь.

Второй день был ещё более насыщенным. В Нью-Йорке действует Центрально-азиатский общественный фонд. Мне позвонил его председатель Ашраф Закиров и попросил дать интервью. Рассказал, что фонд выпускает журнал «Голос Востока» на русском, таджикском и узбекском языках, а кроме того радио- и телепередачи. Несмотря на дальность расстояния от Манхэттена до Бруклина, я не чувствовала усталости и рада была встрече с известным ведущим радио «Голос Востока» Шавкатом Ашти. Он таджик, певец и ведущий концертных мероприятий, живёт уже много лет в Нью-Йорке. Это было его первое интервью по онлайн-радио и телевидению Центрально-азиатского фонда, который в этот день начал своё вещание. А значит, я стала первой гостьей студии.

Про многочисленные ознакомительные поездки и походы по городу рассказывать бы пришлось очень долго. Нью-Йорк за пять дней никак не обойдёшь, но главные достопримечательности мне удалось посетить. По путеводителям Нью-Йорк включает пять районов, расположенных в месте впадения реки Гудзон в Атлантический океан. В центре города расположен густонаселённый Манхэттен – один из крупнейших в мире коммерческих, финансовых и культурных центров. Здесь расположены многочисленные небоскребы, в том числе Эмпайр-стейт-билдинг, и огромный Центральный парк. На залитой неоновыми огнями площади Таймс-сквер расположен театр «Бродвей». Самый посещаемый Комплекс-мемориал 11 сентября. Возведён он в память о жертвах террористического акта, произошедшего на этом месте в 2001 году. Место расположения мемориала также известно как Граунд Зеро. Террористический акт 11 сентября унёс жизни 2 977 человек и стал самым крупным терактом в мировой истории по количеству жертв. И, конечно же, Статуя Свободы, музей Метрополитен, Карнеги-холл, Публичная библиотека, знаменитый Бруклинский мост и бык на Уоллт-стрит, река Гудзон и красивый берег Атлантического океана.

На пятый день меня проводили на поезд, и я отправилась в Вашингтон по приглашению Фархода Салима, посла Республики Таджикистан в Соединённых

Штатах Америки. Прямо на вокзале меня уже ждали друзья, среди них мой коллега – журналист Умед Бабаханов с супругой. Умед, известный в Таджикистане медиамагнат, а главное, интеллигентный и душевный человек. Мне стыдно в этом признаться, но в Душанбе нам не довелось столько общаться, сколько в дни моего пребывания в Вашингтоне. Я познакомилась с прекрасной семьёй Умеда, сыновьями, невесткой, родственниками и друзьями. Они украсили моё пребывание в Вашингтоне и занимали каждую минуту. Особенно его супруга, милая Фируза, которая постоянно звонила, спрашивала, приглашала в гости, показывала мне достопримечательности столицы. Повторяла, что мой визит слишком короткий и надо рационально использовать время.

Презентация книг «Соседушки», «Фарход из Навгилема», «К Востоку устремлён мой взор» и встреча с соотечественниками прошла в нашем посольстве. Я так рада, что в республике воспитали такие дипломатические кадры. Фарход Салим – очень эрудированный и грамотный молодой дипломат. Глядя на него и его коллег, можно уверенно сказать, что у Таджикистана большое будущее!

На встрече был презентован также журнал ОСА MAGAZINE – печатный орган Евразийской творческой гильдии, специально посвященный Северной Америке. Собравшихся заинтересовала статья о посольстве Республики Таджикистан в США и деятельности посла Таджикистана в Соединённых Штатах.

Встреча с читателями прошла очень тепло и непринуждённо. Мне было приятно, что мои книги трогают сердца людей. Особенно запомнились разговоры с землячками Фаридой Асадовой и Шахнозой Якубовой, которые уже много лет живут вдали от родины. На встрече мы подружились с Мариной Абрамс – членом Евразийской творческой гильдии, автором прекрасной книги для детей и юношества «Голубые купола и оранжевые крыши», которую она мне подарила и рассказала, что готовится к печати её английский перевод. На встрече было много вопросов о жизни, семье, творчестве. И я старалась ответить каждому, ведь чувствовала, как искренне радуются моим успехам близкие и друзья.

А в Вашингтоне у меня опять появились две новые подруги Дили – Дилором Баратова и Дилафруз Джураева и пришлось между ними опять загадывать желания. Мы вместе посмотрели три знаменитых здания, где расположены три ветви власти США: Капитолий, Белый дом и здание Верховного суда. А ещё побывали в музее и концертном зале Кеннеди-центра.

Как поётся в песне Вячеслава Бутусова «Гуд бай, Америка!», я очень надеюсь снова вернуться сюда, ведь я оставила здесь среди друзей частичку своего сердца.

РАЗМЫШЛЕНИЯ У ХРАМА ГРОБА ГОСПОДНЯ

Говорят, всё в руках Бога,
и жизнь подтверждает это.

Мне несказанно повезло – получила приглашение из Израиля презентовать мои книги в Тель-Авиве.

Творческий вечер под названием «И душа с душою говорит» организовала президент продюсерского центра ARZ.opera Ирена Арзутова при поддержке Российского культурного центра. Ирена моя юная подруга – член Евразийской творческой гильдии. Они вместе с супругом Сёмой сделали всё для того, чтобы моё пребывание в Израиле стало запоминающимся.

Презентация книг, изданных в Москве и Лондоне, прошла в тёплой и дружественной обстановке. Участники встречи задавали мне – автору много вопросов о Таджикистане и его удивительных людях, о трудном периоде распада СССР, вспыхнувшей гражданской войне в республике в 90-х годах прошлого столетия. Я рассказала о невыдуманных героях моих книг «Город, где сбываются мечты», «Соседушки», «Поделись любовью» и видела в глазах слушателей неподдельный интерес, чувствовала сопереживание. Не остались без внимания и мои научные труды «Сентиментальное путешествие, или Всему своё время» – исследование литературных связей России и Таджикистана 20–30-х годов прошлого столетия и книга о переводах В. А. Жуковского «К Востоку устремлён мой взор». На вечере был показан клип о Душанбе и отрывок из фильма-балета Т. Шахиди «Рубаи Хайяма» с великой балериной Маликой Сабировой. Прима театра оперы Тель-Авива Ирина Бертман исполнила вокальный цикл таджикского композитора Толиба Шахиди.

Но особо меня поразила поездка в священный город Иерусалим – колыбель самых крупных религий мира. Я – мусульманка, Ирена – еврейка, Светлана – христианка стали единым целым. Точно так же, как многочисленные паломники, пришедшие в этот день на Священную землю.

Мы побывали в Александро-Невской лавре, у Стены плача, Белой мечети, в Храме Гроба Господня. Впечатления – не описать!

И знаете, о чём я подумала? Бог-то один, Всемогущий и Человеколюбивый! Он не делит людей на представителей разных религий и конфессий. Бог милостив и всё прощает. Может это испытание для рода человеческого? У Стены плача слышались глухие рыдания, читались молитвы. Все люди писали записки и думали о своём.

Когда я коснулась головой стены, почувствовала, будто мама погладила мой лоб рукой. Чуть ранее в лавре мы вспоминали с Иреной, что мою маму, голубоглазую и белокожую, называли в Душанбе тётей Машей. Я рассказывала подруге о ней. И мама меня услышала. Она приняла моё паломничество. А ведь когда-то мусульмане начинали свой хадж с этого города и до сих пор называют его Байт-ул Мукаддас – Священный город.

Мы долго спускались к Стене плача, день стоял очень жаркий, паломников было много. Обратно по крутым лестницам шли наверх, но усталости не чувствовалось, как будто крылья несли нас назад. Никакой тяжести или одышки, а на сердце покой и духовное умиротворение.

Такое паломничество словно очищение: забываешь свои обиды, всех прощаешь и просишь прощение у Бога.

ИТАЛИЯ: БУХТА ПОЭТОВ И НОВЫЙ ЦЕНТР ВЫСОКОГО ИСКУССТВА

Бухта поэтов – красивейший залив на восточном побережье Лигурии, в городке Леричи. Это одно из самых известных и посещаемых мест в Италии. В первой половине XIX века эти края ещё не были освоены туристами. Прелесть Лигурийского побережья первыми оценили британцы, и прежде всего – люди искусства. В 1820-е годы английские поэты Джордж Гордон Байрон и Перси Биши Шелли поселились здесь.

Вот в этом прекрасном городе – Бухте поэтов, превратившемся в обитель современного музыкального искусства, проводится ежегодный фестиваль классической музыки, хорового пения и музыкально-поэтического искусства.

Какое-то мистическое совпадение или так специально было предусмотрено, но в этот раз мы – участники фестиваля жили на вилле английского поэта-романтика Перси Биши Шелли, где он часто встречался со своим другом поэтом Джорджем Байроном.

С Шелли была жена Мери, автор знаменитого романа «Франкенштейн», с Байроном – его подруга Клер Клермонт.

Сразу на память пришли стихи Шелли:

> Когда лампа разбита,
> Огонь умирает в пыли.
> Когда буря забыта,
> Всё меньше радуг вдали.
> Когда лютня упала,
> Струна звенит всё слабей,
> Когда речь отзвучала,
> Бледнеет память о ней.

Две недели, начиная с 15 августа в Бухте поэтов каждый вечер исполнялись концерты. Основным местом проведения мероприятий стала старинная церковь Святого Франческа, где прошли открытие и закрытие фестиваля, а также большие концерты. Я была поражена заинтересованностью главы города, ответственных работников департаментов, церковных служителей.

На третий день фестиваля исполняли произведения моего мужа Толибхона Шахиди. Весь концерт был посвящён учителю и его ученику – всемирно известному композитору Араму Хачатуряну и его достойному продолжателю Толибу Шахиди. Меня поразило, что все места были заполнены, и многие, кому некуда было сесть, весь концерт стоя слушали музыку. Это было незабываемо!

Состоялась мировая премьера «Концерта для альта и симфонического оркестра» Толиба Шахиди. Солист – альтист-виртуоз Максим Новиков. Дирижёр и главный директор фестиваля Джанлука Марчиано. Были исполнены также фрагменты из балета Толиба Шахиди «Смерть ростовщика». Второе отделение концерта заполнили музыкальные шедевры Арама Хачатуряна.

А после концерта мы решили немного попутешествовать по Италии. Поехали в Пизу посмотреть на знаменитую Пизанскую башню. Пиза – город греческого происхождения. Это определяется строениями церквей и замков. В этом городе как бы «скрываются» многочисленные великолепные башни, исторические здания и прекрасные резиденции.

А рядом Флоренция. Как же не побывать в городе, основанном в I веке до нашей эры! Он насыщен величественными соборами, шикарными виллами и палаццо, зелёными садами и прочими удивительными местами. Незабываемые впечатления – слов нет, чтобы описать это величие! Мне лучше использовать буклеты о тех местах, которые мы успели посетить.

Соборная площадь находится в историческом центре города, на которой торжественно высится здание кафедрального собора Флоренции в окружении колокольни и баптистерия. С давних пор это место вызывает у туристов

возгласы восхищения и самые чистые душевные порывы. Отсюда и стоит прокладывать маршрут своей прогулки по Флоренции.

Мост Понте-Веккьо или же Старый мост – самая почтенная переправа через реку Арно. Одновременно он является главным её украшением. Мост был возведён в XIV веке и до наших дней сохранился в практически неизменном виде. Мост оригинален тем, что с обоих его боков прямо над водой расположились дома.

Церковь Сан-Лоренцо – самая знаменитая флорентийская достопримечательность. Это христианская церковь IV века нашей эры, обновлённая в романском стиле в XI веке. В Средние века её значительным образом реконструировал Брунеллески. В XV столетии шефство над храмом взяло семейство Медичи. Базилика имеет впечатляющее внутреннее убранство, включая белый с золотом потолок, расписной купол и работы лучших зодчих эпохи Ренессанса. Однако наиболее известен этот храм как место упокоения принцев из рода Медичи.

Галерея Уффици находится в десяти минутах ходьбы от площади Синьории. Самостоятельно проложить маршрут до художественной галереи несложно, нужно двигаться по направлению к реке Арно. Средневековый дворец наполнен ценнейшими полотнами итальянских, фламандских и других европейских художников. Основателями картинной галереи стали Медичи, благодаря своим связям и благосостоянию они заполучили настоящие шедевры.

Было желание посмотреть все достопримечательности, но тогда нам нужно было остаться как минимум на десять дней. А такой возможности не было.

Так мы совместили приятное с полезным.

Быть супругой творческого человека, конечно, нелегко. Впервые я услышала эти слова от своей свекрови Мархабохон – жены известного композитора Таджикистана Зиядулло Шахиди. Потом мне ещё раз напомнил об этом педагог моего мужа по консерватории Арам Хачатурян в день нашей первой встречи: «Гуля, мой дорогой цветочек, ты даже не понимаешь, какую петлю на шею накинула. Быть женой настоящего композитора – нелёгкий труд. А Толиб – это неиссякаемый фонтан творчества!» Эти слова я запомнила навсегда. Теперь я сама начала писать художественную прозу и знаю, как важна поддержка родных и близких.

Есть такие моменты в жизни, когда забываешь все трудности и радуешься вместе написанным произведениям. А мне дважды повезло: я не только вижу написанное моим мужем-композитором, но и слушаю его музыку в лучших залах мира.

НОВАЯ ВСТРЕЧА НА РОДИНЕ В. А. ЖУКОВСКОГО

Тридцать пять лет назад я приезжала в Тульскую область в командировку. Работала тогда в Институте языка и литературы им. Рудаки АН Таджикистана, исследовала тему «Жуковский и Восток». Материалов по избранной теме в республике было мало. Пришлось ехать в библиотеки Москвы и Ленинграда, ворошить архивы. Нашла очень ценные факты из биографии и творчества поэта. Захотелось побывать в Тульской области, на родине Василия Андреевича Жуковского – учителя цесаревичей и великого Пушкина. Написала исследовательскую работу о переводческой деятельности Жуковского, связанную с темой Востока. Но опубликовать её не удалось. Лежала она у меня в столе ровно тридцать лет!

Но всему своё время. В 2015 году я издала свою первую повесть «Город, где сбываются мечты». Моя подруга и редактор Вера Дейниченко, узнав, что у меня есть готовая работа о В. Жуковском, настояла на её издании. Ей было очень интересно узнать много нового о своём теперь «земляке». Ведь она жила и работала в городе Суворове Тульской области, рядом с Белёвым – родиной русского поэта и переводчика. В душе моей были сомнения. Но вы не знаете мою подругу! Она просто категорически настояла на издании научно-популярного исследования «К Востоку устремлён мой взор», над которым мы работали с большим азартом и интересом.

А после выхода книги Вера организовала презентацию в районной библиотеке города Суворова. Я с благодарностью приняла приглашение. Собралась целая компания – друзья, бывшие душанбинцы Людмила Синицына, моя соседушка Назокат Холова с дочкой Танечкой. Поехали мы на машине с моим земляком из Ходжента Фаррухом, который сразу подружился со всеми.

Встречали нас как близких друзей. Директор и сотрудники библиотеки как будто всех знали давно. Очень тёплое и искреннее отношение трогало до слёз.

Позже об этой встрече написала моя Вера:

«Ну вот, наконец-то, в городе Суворове Тульской области получили «прописку» не только книги моей подруги – лауреата Евразийской творческой гильдии Гульсифат Шахиди. Она сама приехала на встречу с читателями с группой поддержки – нашими душанбинцами. Это журналист, писатель, фотохудожник Людмила Синицына, гостившая у меня прошлым летом, Назокат Холова, с которой мы работали в Союзе театральных деятелей Таджикистана, с дочкой Таней. А привёз их из Москвы в Суворов водитель и земляк Гули Фаррух Холмурадов – наш верный помощник во всех делах.

Презентация состоялась во Дворце культуры в читальном зале районной библиотеки. Хозяйка её Нелля Сергеевна Меркулова и сотрудники Марина Вячеславовна Зайцева, Марина Николаевна Харькова, Наталья Михайловна Болушкова, Оксана Григорьевна Силаева и Ольга Васильевна Гетце создали удивительную атмосферу какого-то родства душ, благожелательности и доброты.

К выставке книг Гульсифат Шахиди я принесла своё таджикское платье из хан-атласа – подарок подруги. И каждый мог его потрогать, а ещё атласный шарф ручной окраски, сделанный мне в театре моды Центра творческого развития и гуманитарного образования, который стал обложкой для книги о Жуковском «К Востоку устремлён мой взор».

Начали встречу музыкой всемирно известного композитора Толиба Шахиди к фильму «Вперёд, гвардейцы!», и я не удержалась, закружилась в таджикском танце. А потом мои юнкоры разных лет и суворовские читатели рассказывали о своих впечатлениях от прочитанных книг Гульсифат Шахиди. Многие из них полюбили девочку Некбахт из повести «Город, где сбываются мечты», гастарбайтера Абдулваси и олигарха Глеба Николаевича Доброва (прообраз Глеба Дейниченко) из повести «Фарход из Навгилема», жизнерадостную и неунывающую Любашу (все почему-то отметили её сходство со мной) и справедливого фронтовика Григория Семёновича, Фархода и Ширин, Зульфию из повести «Соседушки».

Сколько слов благодарности услышала в свой адрес автор! Гуля порой даже не сдерживала слёзы волнения. Никому не отказала   в автографе – подписывала и дарила книги всем желающим».

Мне как автору было очень приятно, что на встречу со мной пришли и школьники, и студенты. Меня поразили их лица – одухотворённые, открытые, душевные и искренние. Я сразу отметила, что присутствующие не знакомятся впервые с моим творчеством, а уже прочитали все книги и говорили конкретно о темах, героях, событиях, описанных в произведениях. А какие были выступления на встрече! Хочу привести два из них.

Дарья Веселова, студентка Тульского мединститута:

«Мне очень понравился рассказ Гульсифат Шахиди «Красота и Конфуций» из книги «Соседушки». Главная

их героиня – Любовь Владимировна или Любаша, как её ласково называет автор. Мне показалось, что она по характеру и некоторым моментам её жизни очень похожа на нашего педагога по журналистике Веру Владимировну Дейниченко, и даже отчество у неё такое же. Вот, например: «Любаша поражала всех своей жизнерадостностью, умом и добротой. Знала много анекдотов, умела их рассказывать и слыла хохотушкой. У Любаши был сын Сергей, который любил читать книги и писал стихи».

Я знаю, что и у Веры Владимировны есть сын, зовут Сергеем и он тоже пишет стихи. Портретное описание сходно с Верой Владимировной на 100 %. «Она была невысокого роста и очень обаятельная: вздёрнутый носик, ровные красивые зубы и большие синие глаза, которые прямо завораживали. На концерты и спектакли она собиралась такая красивая, что все соседи выходили на неё посмотреть и оценить. Её волнистые русые волосы не требовали ухода и волнами струились по плечам. Расчешет – и прическа готова, как после парикмахерской».

Мне понравилось, что в рассказе много мудрых изречений китайского философа Конфуция. Вот некоторые из них:

«Советы мы принимаем каплями, зато раздаём вёдрами».

«Если ты ненавидишь – значит тебя победили».

«Красота есть во всём, но не всем дано это видеть».

Хочу сказать большое спасибо Гульсифат Гаффоровне за то, что она мне дала возможность познакомиться с таджикским народом и его обычаями».

Инна Сычёва, студентка филфака Московского педуниверситета:

«В новой книге Гульсифат Гаффоровны Шахиди «Фарход из   Навгилема» я сразу отметила для себя одного из героев – олигарха Глеба Николаевича Доброва. Это порядочный и честный человек, который взял на работу таджикских гастарбайтеров и стал для них настоящим другом и помощником в жизни. В самые трудные минуты он поддерживает троих друзей – Абдуласи, Фархода и Фаридуна. Глеб Николаевич умеет разрядить обстановку уместной шуткой, поднимает всем настроение и выручает своих таджикских друзей от нападения подонков-скинхедов. Поэтому автор и придумала ему говорящую фамилию – Добров.

Этот герой напомнил мне мужа Веры Владимировны – поэта Глеба Николаевича Дейниченко. Я не была с ним знакома лично, но многое знаю о нём. И из рассказов Веры Владимировны, и из её книги «Письма к сыну», и из стихотворений самого Глеба Николаевича.

Мы с ребятами в школе «Юнкор» не раз проводили вечера памяти, на которых читали его произведения. Выбирали их сами. И каждый из нас в этих стихах находил себя, свои переживания. И вот одно из знакомых мне стихотворений я увидела на страницах книги Гульсифат Гаффоровны. Его прочёл тот самый олигарх Добров:

Добро всегда прекрасно,
Оно не громогласно.
Тепло и искренне добро,
Уж таково его нутро.
Добра не ищут от добра,
А ждут с утра и до утра.
Добро купить никто не смог,
Ведь у него хозяин – Бог.

Это стихотворение Глеба Николаевича Дейниченко, которое так и называется «Добро». Мне кажется, что оно близко и герою повести, и его прототипу. Ведь Глеб Николаевич, как и олигарх Добров, был человеком весёлым, добрым и отзывчивым.

А теперь я хочу рассказать о заочном знакомстве с Гульсифат Гаффоровной. В прошлом году перед поступлением на филфак Московского педуниверситета я завела свою страничку на «Прозе.ру» и выставила свой первый рассказ «Марш к Победе».

Через несколько дней увидела, что Гульсифат Гаффоровна написала на него мини-рецензию. Было очень приятно прочитать мнение писательницы о моём опусе. Мне кажется, что каждому, кто начинает что-то писать и хочет научиться делать это хорошо, важно услышать комментарии и советы знающих людей».

Вот так, через 35 лет я вновь побывала на родине Василия Андреевича Жуковского. Дух его жив – стремление к Востоку живёт у его земляков и по сей день.

ОТЗЫВЫ И РЕЦЕНЗИИ

ЛИШЬ БЫ
НЕ БЫЛО ВОЙНЫ

О романе В. Медведева «Заххок»

Люблю свой Таджикистан, где горы обнимаются с облаками и целуют небо! Люблю своих соотечественников – красивых, гордых, трудолюбивых, терпеливых, самых добрых на земле. Стараюсь читать всё, что пишут о моей родной стране. Особенно книги тех, кто долго жил и работал с нами рука об руку, плечом к плечу, не жалея своих сил на строительство современной и процветающей республики.

Очень долго читала подаренный мне роман «Заххок» Владимира Медведева. Почувствовала боль автора, его неравнодушие к судьбам людей. Потом ещё раз перечитала, со слезами оглянулась в прошлое. Было тяжело заново вспоминать те события почти 30-летней давности. Книга не для слабонервных. Впечатление, как после просмотра фильма иранского режиссёра Сируса Наврасте «Забивание камнями Сорейи М». Напряжение с первых строк. Как будто машина времени переносит нас в Средневековье. Война всегда страшна, но когда она бессмысленна и против своих, то вдвойне страшна.

Мы – городские видели лишь «цветочки» того противостояния, которое трудно забыть. А книга про

«ягодки», про жестокие схватки бандитов с простыми мирными, порой наивными и непонимающими такой жестокости людьми. Им не понятна дружба головореза с огромной змеёй – питоном, которого для пущей важности и устрашения носит на шее главный злодей романа Зухуршо Хушкадамов. Что от таких жестокосердных можно ждать? Отсюда и выбор названия книги. Заххок – кровожадный правитель из поэмы «Кузнец Кова» эпопеи «Шахнаме» Фирдоуси, подчиняющийся только своим змеям.

«...Поразительно, сколь точный и, главное, современный образ нашёл Фирдоуси. Правитель состоит в симбиозе с рептилиями, вместе с ними питается мозгами подданных. Гениальная метафора, выражающая самую суть власти. Насилие совершается прежде всего над умами подчинённых и лишь во вторую очередь над их телами», – пишет автор.

Да, «случалось такое в Азии – разбойники становились правителями.... Вырезали целые кишлаки, вырезали с изуверской изобретательностью», – рассуждает один из главных героев книги Олег, журналист из Москвы, пока ещё столицы большой страны – СССР.

Интригующее начало с находкой черепа на стройке Андреем, сыном русской Веры и таджика доктора Умара Муродова, развивается до развязки повествования – настоящей отрезанной головы Зухура – Заххока. Так мастерски автор изображает казнь Заххока простым и доверчивым парнем Каримом Тыквой.

Каждая глава – это драматический рассказ от имени

главных персонажей романа. Их всего семь – Андрей, Зарина, Джоруб, Карим Тыква, Олег, Даврон и Эшон Ваххоб. Это хороший приём – вести повествование то от имени мужчины, то от имени женщины. Каждый из них по нескольку раз появляется в 36 главах книги. Все оглавления названы именами действующих лиц, повествующих о событиях в романе. Всем им нелегко – трагедия следует за трагедией, и каждому довелось хлебнуть горя. Зарина, красивая, жизнерадостная и свободолюбивая девочка, не желая быть женой Заххока, обливается бензином и поджигает себя. Даврон – кадровый офицер, который хочет хоть какой-то справедливости и порядка, защищает семью Веры. Он везёт обгоревшую и еле живую Зарину в селение Талхак к знахарке. А потом сам попадает в зиндан (темницу), где видит умирающего журналиста Олега, который не боясь снимал на камеру зверства боевика Зухура Хушкадамова. Этого по задумке автора требовал сюжет романа. Все судьбы героев переплетены.

Сюжетная линия строится на рассказах действующих лиц, рядом с которыми их друзья и враги, родственники и соседи. Сколько имён, сколько географических названий местностей описывается в романе! Таджикские имена и названия автор В. Медведев переводит на русский. Он знает таджикский не по учебникам, он знает язык как его носитель. Со всеми особенностями – пословицами, поговорками, песнями, стихами и даже бранными словами. Он жил среди таджиков много лет, знает обычаи и традиции местного населения, поэто-

му написанному веришь безоговорочно.

Персонажи романа яркие, каждый наделён характерными чертами. Джоруб, Бахшанда, Дильбар, тётушка Кубышка, тётушка Лепёшка, Подшокул-Торба, Саид-бедняк, Ибод, Джав, Джангал, Ёрак, Малах, Сангин, Шер, Дахмарда, Ёдгор, Табар, Зирак, Забардаст, Шокир (Горох), Додихудо, Диловар, Сухроб, Паймон, Саид, дед Мирбобо, Гул, Гадо, Марьям, Махмадали, Гиёз, мулло Раззак, Бахрулло, Сухбат, Занбур, Гафур, мулло Гирдак, Джахонгир, Сангак Сафаров, Файзали Саидов, Алёш и ещё десятки других. Значение многих из имён автор объясняет читателю.

Очень кстати В. Медведев в тексте цитирует стихи соловья Талхака – поэта Валиддина Хирсзода, которого помнят во всём Дарвазе. Не знаешь, то ли это перевод, то ли автор сам сочинил или передал услышанное своими словами, но стилизация очень достоверная:

Если ревности пламя охватит покорную пери,
Берегитесь той девы и люди, и дикие звери.

Или:

Отраднее влачить сундук с песком в пустыне,
Чем матери нести весть скорбную о сыне.

Вызывают эмоциональное напряжение яростные и отчаянные причитания Бахшанды над телом убитого мужа:

О, дом мой, дом мой, без крыши четыре стены.
Царь мой ушёл, остался дутар без струны,
Кувшин без воды, душа без тела,

Дом мой, дом мой, дом опустелый.

Гости пришли – не встанешь,

не скажешь «Салом»,

Заждался тебя твой конь под седлом,

Твоя чаша средь лета покрылась льдом,

Дом мой, дом мой, разрушенный дом.

В таджикском фольклоре есть женские стихи-причитания с рефреном «бе хонумонам». Медведев, конечно же, слышал их и использовал в романе.

Меня поразили пословицы и поговорки, которыми изобилует текст книги В. Медведева. Приведу лишь несколько примеров:

1. Если бы не было носа, один глаз выклевал бы другой – это таджикская пословица «Агар бини набошад, як чашм дигар чашмро кофта мегирад».

2. За нос потянешь – из него душа вон! По-таджикски это «Аз бинниаш гири чонаш мебарояд»

3. У кривого и тень кривая. Это русский перевод таджикской пословицы «Одами качро сояш хам кач мешавад».

4. Крыша одна – погоды две, таджикский аналог «Як бому ду хаво».

И таких примеров можно привести десятки! Богатый материал для языковедов, фольклористов и краеведов. По географическим названиям кишлаков, рек, ущелий и даже развилок можно нарисовать карту этой горной области Таджикистана – от Дарваза до Кала-

и-Хумбы: Талхак, Вазирон, Ворух, Ватан, Дараи шур, Дараи Гургон, гора Сарбиён, хребет Хазрати Хусейн, река Ях-Су, озеро Осмон-куль и ещё сотни названий.

Именно такое отношение к материалу даёт повод верить автору, что он не выдумывал, не преувеличивал, не писал по сводкам, а сам был свидетелем тех событий. Его даже можно представить в образе журналиста Олега, который стал невольным участником этой жуткой войны. Перед командировкой он переживал и много рассуждал:

«Я с ужасом следил за событиями. Издали. По газетам, радио и телевидению. Один мой товарищ, проживший в Таджикистане много лет, насмотревшись телевизионных репортажей, как-то воскликнул: «Мы-то всегда считали, что таджики – удивительно красивый народ! Мягкий, доброжелательный, трудолюбивый, весёлый. Откуда у них патологическая жестокость? Выходит, они совсем не такие, какими казались...» Он был несправедлив. Убивали не трудолюбивые и весёлые. Это их убивали.

«А ты вспомни нашу гражданскую войну, – ответил я. – Лютовали не меньше, а то, пожалуй, поболее. Во время катаклизмов всегда всплывают на поверхность садисты, психопаты, прирождённые убийцы».

И с этими словами я полностью согласна. Владимир Медведев показал личное отношение к событиям в Таджикистане и дал свою объективную оценку. Книга его о том, чтобы помнить это бессмысленное противостояние, чтобы ценить мир. Было сложно и после войны: без хлеба, без тепла, без света, без мужчин – кто погиб, кто уехал на заработки. И многие терпели и верили, что всё будет хорошо.

Лишь бы не было войны...

КОГДА МЕЧТЫ СБЫВАЮТСЯ

Вышла в свет книга Зауре Турехановой «Амина Туран в стране номадов», выпущенная алма-атинским издательством «Алматыкитап баспаси». Хочу поздравить автора. Книга настолько национальна и самобытна, что, читая её, узнаёшь о мифологии и фольклоре казахского народа, открываешь для себя много интересного.

Зауре, несмотря на молодость, признанный автор, она лауреат престижных премий Казахстана. За книгу об Алма-ате стала дипломантом на книжном фестивале в Лондоне. Познакомились мы с ней именно на этом форуме. Очень уверенная презентация, которая показала прекрасное знание материала исследования древнего города. Приятно было, что дочь поддерживала мама – очаровательная Зульфия-ханум.

Именно тогда Зауре рассказала мне о другой своей книге, которая готовилась к печати на русском языке – «Амина Туран в стране номадов», чем-то перекликаясь по названию с «Алисой в стране чудес». Она мечтала, что сможет передать своему читателю всю красоту казахского мифологического эпоса и фольклора. Книгу автор посвятила своему любимому дедушке Молдагали Берджанову.

Книга легко читается, хоть и объёмная для того круга читателей, кому предназначена. Дети будут возвращаться к каждой главе, причём с удовольствием – сразу прочесть это им будет сложно. Но именно увлекательный стиль книги будет их возвращать к необычайным приключениям прекрасной девочки Амины. Ей всего двенадцать лет, но её силе и мудрости может позавидовать взрослый.

Каждое новое испытание, которое должна пройти Амина, – это путь к счастью её народа, людей, отчаявшихся и надеющихся только на её смелость и смекалку.

Все двадцать глав книги – это новое приключение Амины. Об этом говорит Айдахар-кампир перед приключениями и ведёт девочку по пути к цели:

– Я пошлю ей испытание, чтобы проверить силу её воли и доброту сердца. Если она та, кто нам нужен, то девочка, без сомнения, с этой миссией, с любой неразрешимой задачей справится.

Автор словами своего персонажа говорит о вечных истинах:

– Ведь нужно смотреть не на возраст, а на то, что в душе и на совести человека.

И только если у этой девочки появиться желание творить добро и помогать людям, мифические персонажи дадут ей шанс, проверив её на деле и поверив в её благородство. Каждое её путешествие – это новое испытание.

Отважной девочке Амине с её добрым и отзывчивым сердцем удаётся пройти все трудности и прспят-

ствия в пути. Это джинн, чёрный чародей, великаны Зардахши, колдунья Карга и другие.

Амина выполняет своё предназначение – находит Книгу судеб, чтобы спасти жителей городов-пиал, которым без этой священной книги не выжить.

«Как известно, если творишь добро, то это возвращается к тебе ответным добром, а если ты творишь зло, то оно, усиливаясь, непременно возвращается», – говорит Зауре Туреханова словами своего персонажа.

Вся книга пронизана ощущением любви и добра к своей истории, мифологии, народным сказаниям, она предназначена для детей и юношества и написана в жанре детско-юношеского романа-фэнтези, её полезно почитать взрослым.

Мечты сбываются, когда в них веришь и стремишься к совершенству – об этом книга Зауре Турехановой.

«ВСЁ, КИНА НЕ БУДЕТ!»

*Записки на полях книги
Мухиддина Махмудова*

«Кино Бако Садыкова»

Не зря я вспомнила слова героя фильма «Джентльмены удачи». Но здесь хочется применить её в прямом смысле. Большое количество выпущенных перед перестройкой картин или по утверждению автора в эпоху Безвременья, были обречены на «полочное забвение». Тратились большие деньги, технические и человеческие ресурсы, а в итоге картина оказывалась на полке – «всё, кина не будет!»

Но время показало, что лучшее кино всё же находит своего зрителя и понимание среди поклонников, а не конъюнктуры. Прочитав книгу Мухиддина Махмудова, я пришла к выводу, что Бако Садыков, несмотря на преграды, препоны, а порой непонимание в своём окружении, всё равно счастливый человек. Он смог самовыразиться, создать прекрасные полотна, придать им специфический суфийский колорит. Я не киновед, не кинокритик, а лишь обычный зритель, и поэтому писать научную или аналитическую статью не смогла бы. Эти заметки – лишь моё восприятие автора через кар-

тины его героя. Мне могут возразить, автор – истинный поклонник и преданный друг, поэтому вся книга субъективно-положительная. Отвечу: пусть о каждом настоящем творческом человеке ТАК пишут поклонники и коллеги! Это их право.

Бако Садыков не ординарен. Понять язык его кино совсем не просто. С первого фильма «Адонис XIV», который «полных десять лет был фактически под арестом», никого не оставил равнодушным. Фильм, на мой взгляд, о человеческом тщеславии в форме притчи и символики. Оказывается, что режиссёр и не мог по-другому мыслить. Он не искал лёгкого пути в творчестве. Последующие его работы – тому доказательство. Как писала киновед Лутфия Айни, «во всём вкус старой притчи».

Режиссёр не только увлечён идеями суфизма, он передаёт образы и притчи, вдохновившими его от прочтения лучших образцов из творчества поэтов-суфиев Руми, Саной, Аттара.

Прежде чем написать отзыв о книге, я посмотрела, что же есть о Бако Садыкове в Интернете. Такая уж теперь привычка наработалась. В Гугле 14 страниц только сносок публикаций о жизни и творчестве режиссёра, статьи и отзывы о его работах, выдержки из статей. Первым делом посмотрела Википедию и Кинопоиск, где перечислены все киноработы режиссёра. В Ютюбе только «Адонис XIV».

Но моя задача рассказать о книге Мухиддина Махмудова. Это сборник статей, интервью, либретто, киносценариев и большого количества писем из архива Бако Садыкова. Хочу отметить, что такое разнообразие выбора архивно-документального материала, множество фотографий и комментариев не сделали книгу трудной и пёстрой для чтения. Её за один присест не прочитаешь, приходится возвращаться. И хотя книга рассчитана на широкий круг читателей, в первую очередь она будет интересна коллегам и специалистам по истории советского и постсоветского кино.

Спасибо автору за то, что подарил мне эту книгу, иначе где бы я её нашла? Теперь я редко бываю на Родине, но читаю всё, что пишут о нашем крае, о людях, которые немало сделали для развития таджикского искусства и пропаганды его на международном уровне.

Мухиддин Махмудов с большим уважением относится к герою своей книги. Вместе с ним радуется его успехам и творческим находкам, переживает за непонимание и порой неприятие окружением его принципиальных творческих позиций. Автор приводит цитату о картине «Благословенная Бухара» из статьи Дж. Рахматова «Когда небо дымилось, но не загорелось» (газета «Адабиёт ва санъат» – «Литература и искусство» от 13 июня 1991 года). Вот эти строки:

«Однако восточные люди восприняли этот фильм с воодушевлением, так как в нём нашла отражение боль нации. Она, как улочки Бухары, достаточно извилиста, однако не беспросветна. После каждой улочки появляется новый проход. Думаете, конец света, всё, тупик, но

вдруг открывается новый просвет, иные переходы. И человек, облегчённо вздохнув, открывает для себя новый мир. И так без конца. Если один в кирпиче видит строительный материал, другой – орудие для удара, то Бако Садыков видит в нём горсть земли предков».

Собирая такой богатый материал о жизни и творчестве режиссёра, Мухиддин Махмудов объял необъятное. Всё это можно было издать в нескольких книгах! А тут всего четыреста страниц, которые прекрасно сложились в почти энциклопедическое издание. Книга легко читается и нет ощущения переизбытка и нагромождённости фактами и материалом.

Творческие люди, особенно талантливые, всегда окружены не только почитателями, понимающими тебя коллегами и друзьями. Есть и оппоненты. Без этого нет жизни у настоящего художника. Мне это известно не понаслышке. Будучи супругой известного и талантливого композитора и начав свою творческую деятельность, я поняла, что, наверное, зависть и слухи закаляют нас и делают сильнее.

Условности держат иногда идею, как птицу в клетке, но она находит дорогу к свободе и парит высоко в облаках. Хочется привести суфийскую притчу от Руми, которая подтверждает сказанное.

ПОРУЧЕНИЕ ПОПУГАЯ

Один купец, известный также тем, что владел учёным попугаем, как-то по торговым делам собрался в

Индостан. Перед тем как отправиться в путь, он спросил всех своих чад и домочадцев, кто и какой хотел бы получить подарок из далёкого края. И каждый из них высказал своё пожелание. Спрошен был купцом и попугай, который попросил хозяина:

– Когда ты придёшь в мой отчий край, скажи всем попугаям Индостана, что меня терзает разлука с ними, что я постоянно о них думаю в своей неволе, и скажи, что я от них жду совета, как мне совладать со своей печалью. Ведь где-то живёт и мой пестрокрылый кумир, моя милая, мы с ней были, как Лейли и Меджнун, и теперь я вспоминаю её с любовью. Пусть же, получив от меня весть, будет меня вспоминать и она, и пусть она в час веселья в память обо мне обронит слезу.

Купец поклялся исполнить просьбу попугая, и когда он, прибыв в Индостан, увидел там столько счастливых птиц, он сразу же вспомнил свою клятву и в точности передал слова птицы. Когда он закончил перед ними свой рассказ, один из попугаев громко воскликнул и упал замертво, распростёрши свои обессиленные крылья. Купец же почувствовал себя виновным в смерти птицы и долго ругал себя за то, что дал волю словам и так точно пересказал то, что ему говорил его собственный попугай.

Между тем его торговые дела подошли к своему завершению, и он, закупив обещанные подарки, двинулся в обратный путь. Когда он вернулся, попугай спросил его:

– Выполнил ли ты мою просьбу?

– Выполнить-то я её выполнил, но теперь и сам каюсь, что это сделал. Дело в том, что как только я рассказал птицам, как ты здесь томишься, одна из птиц из сострадания так расстроилась, что упала замертво, и ни я, ни другие птицы ей не могли помочь.

Как только учёный попугай услышал этот рассказ, он внезапно поник головой и упал на дно своей золочёной клетки. Там он затрепетал и замер так же странно, как и его индостанский сородич. Увидев, что птица умерла, её хозяин в горе сорвал с себя чалму, стал рвать на себе одежду и причитать:

– Ты был так сладкоголос! Зачем же ты такое с собой сделал? Неужели мне теперь вовек не услышать твоё пение и твои речи? Неужели я тебя не верну к жизни? Ведь таких, как ты, не было даже в садах царя Соломона!

В таких вот причитаниях и слезах купец провёл целый день и только к вечеру угомонился, вынес клетку в сад и бережно выложил из неё мёртвую птицу. Но попугай, почувствовав себя на свободе, вдруг ожил, раскрыл глаза и вспорхнул на ветку.

Увидев это, купец сначала остолбенел, а потом вскричал:

– Как же ты додумался до этой уловки? Неужели я сам, о том не зная, привёз тебе из Индостана совет твоих собратьев?

– Ты принёс мне весть от моих братьев, – отвечал попугай. – Они через тебя мне сказали, чтобы я перестал услаждать людей пением, потому что, чем оно звонче

и мелодичнее, тем прочней запоры на клетке, а мой брат ещё дал мне совет притвориться мёртвым, чтобы обрести свободу. Прощай же, мой хозяин! Я никогда не забуду, что освободился благодаря тебе!

Купец задумался над словами попугая и сказал:

– Пусть Господь хранит тебя, ибо своим поступком ты приблизил меня к пониманию Истины. Спасибо тебе за урок! А теперь прощай и лети к своей истинной Любви!

Но не притчей хотелось бы закончить мои авторские размышления. А выдержкой из письма Бако Садыкова к журналистке Тамаре Хетагуровой:

«Жизнь продолжается, меня вдохновляет в этой жизни интерес к ней, всё, что меня окружает – моя любимая Зубейда, мои сыновья, внуки и невестка».

Вот оно истинное счастье! И об этом книга Мухиддина Махмудова.

ДИЛЯРА ЛИНДСЕЙ: «Я НАУЧИЛАСЬ ЗВУКАМ ДОВЕРЯТЬ...»

Знакомьтесь, новое имя в мире книг – Диляра Линдсей. В Лондоне в издательстве «Хердфоршир Пресс» в 2017 года вышел её сборник стихов и новелл «Музыка между строк». Диляра по-настоящему евразийский автор. Казахская писательница из Лондона, родившаяся в Ташкенте и пишущая на русском языке.

Знаю Диляру уже несколько лет. На презентациях в Лондоне она выступала с отзывами о моих книгах «Город, где сбываются мечты» и «Соседушки». Она не просто высказывала свои впечатления о произведениях, но и делала объективный анализ изображения героев и ситуаций, отмечая лёгкость и образность текстов.

Когда мне предложили сделать отзыв на первую книгу Диляры, я не задумываясь согласилась. Она много лет писала в стол, так как была не уверена в своих творческих возможностях. А ведь книга получилась! Я заметила, как точна Диляра в выражении образов стихотворной лирики. Даже некоторая пафосность, где-то нестыковка с размером или рифмой делается автором осознанно. А искренность и задушевность затмевает многое.

Сборник стихов и прозы Диляра посвящает своим «любимым родителям, единственному сыну – Человеку Нового Времени и ушедшему в мир иной супругу». Она пишет в предисловии:

«Я принадлежу к поколению людей, которые волею судеб стали свидетелями распада огромной Советской страны. В периоде «до» осталось счастливое яркое детство и долгое, длиною в 21 год, музыкальное образование».

Я выбрала это признание автора не случайно, так как поняла: музыка, несмотря на все повороты жизни, осталась основополагающим звеном в жизни и творчестве Диляры Линдсей. Поэтому и назвала она свою книгу «Музыка между строк». И стихи, и новеллы автора полны звучания:

> Ведомая желанием познать
> Закон божественной гармонии,
> Я научилась звукам доверять
> И слышать душ иных симфонии...

Диляра смотрит на жизнь, как музыкант, хотя давно поменяла профессию:

> Открылись тайны многие мне постепенно
> О том, что каждый человек он словно инструмент
> В большом оркестре жизни бренной,
> Назначена ему своя мелодия и свой момент...

Диляра признаётся, что благодаря своему профессиональному музыкальному образованию состоялась как личность, научилась мыслить и чувствовать органично, образно и масштабно. И настоящую любовь она познала именно через высокое искусство музыки:

> Меня с тобою музыка свела,
> Узором нот мне выстлала дорогу,
> Звезду любви аккордами зажгла
> И привела к душе твоей порогу...

К собственному творчеству автор относится очень ответственно, хотя и признаёт, что она не оригинальна. Как стихотворец она очень скромна и непритязательна, ищет выход своим нежным и искренним чувствам:

> Уж изданы давно все лучшие поэты,
> И песни лучшие, пожалуй, сложены,
> Но тянется рука писать сонеты
> И рифмовать признания в любви!
> Открой и ты в себе источник вдохновенья,
> Пленяясь лабиринтами судьбы,
> Ищи себя, не уставая верить
> В победу всеобъемлющей Любви!

Проза Динары Линдсей отличается от поэзии своим фактологическим, краеведческим и автобиографическим материалом. Но это совсем не наукообразная, а вполне творческая попытка автора рассказать о своих путешествиях.

Первая новелла называется «Джайляу вечных пионеров». Джайляу – это стоянка кочевников, роль которых исполняют «вечные пионеры» – группа друзей-романтиков. Они превращают время отпуска в активный отдых под названием «пионерская зарница». Главный зачинщик и организатор Константин со своей многочисленной семьёй и друзьями ежегодно проводит такой праздник души. И выезд в августе в юрту стал традиционным.

«Чтобы в который раз напиться прозрачного горного воздуха и по-хорошему отравиться всей той неописуемой красотой и благодатью альпийских лугов, да и наполниться мощным зарядом роскошного человеческого общения под сводами капризного тянь-шаньского неба», так автор определяет цель.

И опять музыкальное заключение:

«Всё хорошее когда-нибудь подходит к концу, и вот наступает заключительный день летнего праздника. Сколько помню, день этот выдаётся яркий, солнечный, особенный. Он как финал большой мажорной симфонии громко подводит итог всему...»

Рассказ ведётся от имени автора, поэтому всему веришь и вместе с ней переживаешь все моменты её летней сказки, которая радует память целый год. Славная традиция входит в историю и продолжается вновь и вновь.

Вторая новелла отмечена автором, как отрывки из повести «Одиссеи Сеньора Саласара или приключения английского номада».

Это отрывок из биографии Диляры Линдсей. Маленькая счастливая история из жизни, по настроению автора это очень заметно. Повествование также ведётся от имени Диляры. Во втором этапе жизни музыка переходит в поэзию и прозу жизни. Казахстан, Южная Африка, Англия – кочевая жизнь автора и главного героя.

«Позже, когда мы стали кочевать вместе, он любил повторять:

– Моя жизнь – это настоящее приключение без финала! Я бы ни за что не поменял оседлую размеренную жизнь на то, что я имею...

...Отпуск? Что вы имеете в виду? У меня вся жизнь – отпуск! Я только и делаю, что путешествую и наслаждаюсь жизнью!»

Диляра в этой новелле подробно рассказывает о биографии героя: кто он, откуда, кто его родственники, как он стал ездить по разным странам и превратился в полиглота, изучая многие европейские языки. А с какой любовью описана встреча со второй половинкой и последние минуты прощания с любимым навсегда:

«Наверное, в тот момент под звуки любимой музыки светлая душа Саласара уносилась в сказочный рай его детства. Где она будет жить вечно, купаясь в ласковых лучах вечно золотого солнца, среди крошечных сказочных птичек колибри и опьяняющего аромата цветущих апельсиновых аллей...»

Я уверена, что поэзия и проза евразийской писательницы Диляры Линдсей найдёт место в сердцах многих читателей. «Музыка между строк» – её первая книга и во многом пробная. Будут ещё   и другие издания, я в этом уверена.

«ТАДЖИКИ ИДУТ»
Умеда Бабаханова

Долго думала, как назвать свой отзыв о книге Умеда Бабаханова, которая увидела свет в 2012 году в душанбинском издательстве «Эр-граф». Автор подарил мне её совсем недавно. И решила оставить как есть – «Таджики идут».

Сколько значений в этом названии! И хотя оно взято из конкретной статьи, но очень удачно подходит ко всему сборнику. Таджики в лице автора идут по необъятным просторам земли, заявляя о себе как о народе, сумевшем покорить сердца миллионов людей. Это люди Таджикистана – уникальной страны, прошедшей немало испытаний временем. Но народ остался таким же добрым, гостеприимным, с мироощущением, определённым веками.

Так я могу сказать и об авторе книги, который даже самые страшные страницы новейшей истории Таджикистана описывает очень сдержанно и объективно. Интеллигентность – вот основная черта характера У. Бабаханова. И это имеет свои корни.

В таджикском языке есть мудрая поговорка: «Мероси падар хохи, касби падар омуз!», что означает «Хочешь получить наследство отца – учись его профессии». Умед Бабаханов живой пример тому. Он посвящает свою книгу Мансуру Бабаханову – отцу, учителю и другу.

Я знала отца Умеда. Это был известный историк, политолог и исследователь. Я поражалась его богатому интеллекту и умению говорить очень спокойно, без лишних эмоций. Он умел выслушивать и, не навязывая своего мнения, объяснял и спокойно рассуждал вслух, убеждая собеседника. Это талант! Мансур Бабаханов не любил пустых споров. Всё называл своими именами. И никогда никто не мог уйти от него обиженным или недовольным. А люди-то разные! Он оставил много достойных трудов после себя, но главное богатство его жизни – дети Умед и Фируза.

Почему я вспомнила о Мансуре Бабаханове? Читая книгу его сына, я невольно убеждалась в том, что он рядом с ним везде и повсюду. Его интеллигентность передалась не только Умеду – человеку, но и как журналисту. Я думаю, что сын, имея такой багаж, обязательно станет талантливым писателем. Хотя и в медиа-бизнесе Умед показал себя с самой лучшей стороны. Газета «Азия плюс», с которой он начинал свой бизнес, по опросам, уже много лет занимает первые строчки рейтингов по популярности. Теперь это огромный медиа-холдинг.

Учился Умед Бабаханов на востоковеда и, как сам признаётся, «никогда не планировал стать журналистом». Имел хорошую перспективу на дипломатическом поприще, ведь лучшие выпускники факультета востоковедения Таджикского госуниверситста обяза-

тельно становились прекрасными переводчиками. Они получали возможность работать в ближневосточных дипкорпусах. Но Умед выбрал иной путь. Перестройка дала ему крылья. Он верил во всё новое и решил после армии вернуться в Таджикистан и служить в «прекрасное и наивное время» на благо Родины. Начал он свою трудовую деятельность корреспондентом республиканской газеты «Комсомолец Таджикистана» и понял – это его стезя. С того времени прошло уже более 25 лет. И он каждый раз доказывает и себе, и другим, что выбрал правильный путь.

Мне сразу стало понятно, почему свой сборник Умед открыл статьёй «Таджики идут». Этот первый материал будущего маститого журналиста даёт импульс всей книге. Взрослое поколение таджикистанцев помнит инициативу студентки Душанбинского пединститута Муниры Набиевой о виртуальном Поясе мира – 39-й параллели, на которой лежит Таджикистан. На этом же поясе находятся Греция, Италия, Испания, США, Северная Корея и другие страны, и Мунира предложила «дружить домами». Дружить и жить в мире… Но как сознаётся автор, «перестройка – наивная эпоха».

Сложные годы распада Советского Союза больнее всего ударили по Таджикистану. Хотя многим республикам пришлось пережить этот болезненный переходный период истории когда-то огромной страны. Поэтому автор посвятил этой теме четыре большие главы книги – «Предчувствие беды», «Хроника безумия», «Командировка в Афганистан» и «Война». И названия его статей полностью резюмируют всё написанное о войне в Таджикистане: «Одни стреляют, другие уезжают», «Куда ни глянь – везде кровь», «Наверное, мы все сошли с ума», «Не трогайте мой дом, я ещё вернусь», «Гуляя по Душанбе, не задень плечом боевика», «В зоопарках тихо умирают слоны», «Ветви власти вырастают из ствола автомата» и другие. Умед Бабаханов в то тревожное время уже был опытным журналистом – специальным корреспондентом газеты «Комсомольская правда» и свидетелем всего происходящего. Автор приводит слова своего героя: «Если есть день Страшного суда, то мы его видели». Это уже   о беженцах, которым пришлось перейти границу Афганистана.

Независимость Таджикистану далась через тяжкие испытания. И прав автор: «У таджикского слова «озоди» – свобода оказался солоноватый привкус – привкус слёз и крови». Не каждый готов был принять время, когда свобода приходит неожиданно. С верой на победу разума радуется Умед подписанию мирного договора между противоборствующими сторонами, тому, что в Таджикистане у людей постепенно налаживается жизнь. Называет он эту главу «Новый век. Новые надежды и разочарования». Главным лейтмотивом здесь я бы выделила вопрос автора «Нужно ли нам покаяние?» И он прав, считая, надо работать над ошибками, понимать друг друга, быть начеку, чтобы никогда не повторилось такое испытание, как гражданская братоубийственная война. И созидать новый Таджикистан. А это нелегко – строить дороги и мосты, туннели и гидроэлектростанции.

Умед Бабаханов побывал во многих странах. Это Россия, Казахстан, Афганистан, Чехия, Китай, а также Япония, Англия, Швейцария, Германия, Южная Корея. Все перечислять не стану. Читая статьи о его поездках и впечатлениях, я пришла к выводу, что он прекрасно разбирается в политике. И опытный дипломат в оценках. Всё очень корректно и убедительно. Сдержанная критика, умеренный пафос, доказательные умозаключения. Он прекрасно разбирается в объекте описания, и ему доверяешь. Ничего лишнего. Текст легко читается и воспринимается.

Я не люблю политику, может, потому, что многого не могу понять. Уже давно политика – «управляемый хаос», и аналитики, и журналисты все обсуждают эту «аксиому», а мне это не даёт покоя. Получается, нам очень трудно определиться, ведь рядом СИЛЬНЫЕ МИРА СЕГО?!. Нет, политика – это не для меня! А вот У. Бабаханов пишет об этом с осознанием проблемы.

В статье «Демократы всех стран, объединяйтесь!» о международном форуме в Сеуле автор называет его «большой тусовкой» главных демократов мира. Его как гражданина волнует, «кто будет определять, какая страна развивает демократию, а какая идёт вспять, к диктатуре».

Умед Бабаханов – участник саммитов и член многих правительственных делегаций по налаживанию сотрудничества и дипломатических отношений. Рассказывает об этом вскользь и, не акцентируя внимание на себе. Всё у него сдержанно, чётко и скромно. С прези-

дентом страны Эмомали Рахмоном, с членами делегации он «прорубает окно в Европу», посещая Францию, подробно описывая встречу Эмомали Рахмона с Жаком Шираком. Из Франции вылетают в Америку, где проходят встречи с представителями деловых кругов. Автор называет эти визиты «историческими». Дальше – Бельгия и Германия. И везде главный вопрос – стремление к сотрудничеству и осуществление взаимных интересов.

В книге есть и научные статьи. Хочу особо выделить исследование «Реформа таджикской письменности: как это было», где автор скрупулёзно изучает процесс тройного перехода таджикского алфавита с арабского на латинский, и с латинского на кириллицу. Автор приводит примеры сложности китайского и японского алфавита. Несмотря на это, ни Китай, ни Япония не поменяли свою письменность. А ведь у нас меняли арабское письмо якобы из-за его сложности, используя как фактор, влияющий на уровень грамотности народа. Умед приводит много фактов из истории изменения письменности. И сожалеет, что уже несколько поколений наших соотечественников не могут читать богатую таджикско-персидскую литературу и исторические источники в подлиннике. И я с автором полностью согласна.

В книге немало актуальных интервью с интересными людьми. Кроме того, автор часто цитирует высказывания таджикских поэтов и писателей И первый из них Садриддин Айни – основоположник таджикской советской литературы.

Меня привлекло интервью с известным немецким востоковедом Манфредом Лоренцем – этим не каждый журналист может похвастаться. Научные труды М. Лоренца о таджикском языке и литературе популярны в исследовательских кругах ориенталистов Европы. Собеседниками Умеда Бабаханова были такие известные личности, как Джордж Сорос, Ахмадшо Маъсуд, посол РФ в Таджикистане Максим Пешков, деятели кино Давлат Худоназаров и Валерий Ахадов, писатель Тимур Зульфикаров и другие.

Все интервью интересны и познавательны. К примеру, «Муравей Варзобского ущелья» – это о Тимуре Зульфикарове, «...его называют самым христианским и самым мусульманским, самым эротическим и самым аскетическим». Интервью посвящено 70-летию известного поэта и писателя.

«Моя литература, как дикий виноград, который сам по себе, без химикатов сладок», – говорит о своём творчестве Тимур Касымович.

Но мне особенно нравятся его высказывания о судьбе: «Человек вышел из рая и идёт туда обратно. Великие смиренники идут в рай. Ад есть только на земле». И ещё – «Настоящий Поэт всегда одинок. Но любой одинокий мудрец всегда ждёт и прислушивается: не постучится ли кто в дверь его одинокой кибитки...»

Пересказать сборник статей Умеда Бабаханова «Таджики идут» – это дело невозможное. Книгу надо читать. Издана она небольшим тиражом и передаётся из рук в руки.

А я желаю автору дальнейших успехов в творчестве. Верю в его писательский дар.

276

КУВШИН ЖЕНСКИХ МЕЛОДИЙ РАУШАН

В московском издательстве «Художественная литература» вышла в свет новая книга Раушан Буркитбаевой-Нукеновой «Завитки каракуля. Избранное». Автор послесловия, директор издательства академик Георгий Пряхин отметил: «Я давно не читал в современной восточной женской поэзии ничего более откровенного, чувственного и трагичного, как в стихах Раушан».

Поэзия – взвесь заколдованных снов.
И критик оценит мой странный улов.

Есть таджикская пословица «Исмаш ба чисмаш мувофик», которая в переводе звучит так: имя соответствует внутреннему и внешнему облику человека. Бывает, люди в совместно прожитых годах становятся не только не похожими, но иногда и вовсе не соответствуют своему имени. Но только не Раушан. Родители угадали её имя точно.

Раушан от таджикского слова «Равшан», что означает светлая, яркая, лучезарная, иногда в контексте – открытая, тёплая и понятная. Казахстанская русскоязычная поэтесса Раушан Буркитбаева-Нукенова, знакомая читателям многих стран благодаря переводам, имеет много наград и большое признание среди своих читателей.

Мы с ней в чём-то похожи. Я тоже пишу на русском. Мне также близка тема любви к родному краю, к своему народу, друзьям. Понятна тоска по прошлому и несбыточному. Но она поэт, который видит иногда насквозь и замечает всё:

> ...Когда же град воспоминаний
> Вдруг сердце скосит наповал,
> Ты извлеки из подсознанья
> Летящий в бездну перевал,
> Внизу которого по-прежнему
> Несётся бурная река,
> Где столько радости и нежности
> Дарила нежная рука.

Врач по специальности, врачеватель по своей поэзии, Раушан многогранна в творчестве. А главное в нём – это звук, иногда задорный, радостный, но в основном задушевное монотонное остенато, задумчивое и грустное. Именно такие звуки мы все слышали от своих родственников, когда они пели колыбельные.

> Не ломай мою душу, не надо...
> И сквозь крики запруженных улиц
> Вырвусь я через прутья ограды
> И от яркого света зажмурюсь.
> И мелодии чистые звуки

Зазвучат в этот час, как с экрана,
И нахлынут волной сквозь разлуку
В пересохшее горло фонтана.

Поэзия Центральной Азии во многом похожа своим разнообразием тем и сюжетов, многозвучием и красочностью. Тому, кто хоть раз побывал в этих красивых и необычайных азиатских уголках и увидел непохожую на другие страны землю могучих гор и бескрайних просторов, станет понятна музыка стихов Раушан:

Эфира музыку услышать в гнетущей тишине...
мелодия ночи в пучину уводила.

«Музыка линий» – так называется раздел стихов Раушан. Здесь и «Лунная соната», и отдельные стихи, посвящённые Бетховену: «Ты наполнял без устали твореньем совершенным, как свет, пронзая тьму, бессмертный человек!»
О Бахе Раушан говорит:

Плодовитый отец мессы пишет и фуги.
В музыкальный ларец – цикл прелюдий для вьюги.

А вот о другом композиторе: «Венгерский танец – фееричный Брамс! И в пляс пошёл народ под эти звуки...»
И всё это – Парадиз музыки:

Молча покинув глубины шкатулки,
В объятьях свободы и темноты,
Музыка бродит по закоулкам
И заполняет тоннель пустоты…

Музыка стихов Раушан полна любви, чувств и желаний, но в ней угадывается и светлая грусть, это особенно трогает душу, ведь не бывает любви без печали:

Нет подруги, кроме вьюги,
Ей всё можно рассказать,
Про любимого мужчину,
Про тоску и про кручину
Будем вместе завывать.

Но грусть-тоска не заставляет печалиться, она светла и дарит теплоту. Она лишь откровенно говорит о жизни такой, какова она есть, и учит нас многому:

Я не забуду миг счастливый,
Когда душистой и цветущей сливой
Наполнился мой душный кабинет.
Тебя, увы, давно уж рядом нет,
Лишь аромат духов остался.

Раушан принимает любовь с улыбкой, в чувствах она всегда честна и открыта. Этому училась у Валерия Брюсова, Константина Бальмонта, Иосифа Бродского, Осипа Мандельштама, Бориса Пастернака, Анны Ахматовой, Беллы Ахмадуллиной и Олжаса Сулейменова.

Раушан не сидит на месте. Она вечный странник. Погружаясь в её стихотворения, вместе с автором мы то в родном ауле, то в Чимбулаке, то в живописном месте Кок-Тобе. А потом мы уже путешествуем по миру – Самарканд, Москва, Лондон, Санкт-Петербург, Париж. И всё же, по словам поэта, «в собственном доме мы иностранцы»:

Дети – на Запад, а мы – на Восток,
В разных краях мы ищем исток.

Какие дороги нам предначертаны судьбой? Как распорядится нами Вселенная? Ответ Раушан находит у Льва Гумилёва: «В каждом из нас живёт генетическая память, не ощущаемая в повседневности, но иногда вспыхивающая в подсознании…»
Над этим стоит задуматься:

Куда несёт тебя судьба?
Шаманский катыш, что подскажет?
Вот к Иртышу бежит Ульба,
И Млечный путь маршрут покажет.
Как хрупок наш стеклянный мир,
Не крепче мамонтовой плоти.
И краток наш вселенский пир,
И где-то рок незримый бродит.

Как хорошо сказал в предисловии книги Дюсенбек Накипов: «…И хотя Раушан, как и все мы, живёт среди житейских тревог и проблем и разнонастроенных оркестров современного мира, она противится резким нотам порицания, а ведёт свой поиск утерянной гармонии, ибо её внутреннее авторское кредо – это музыка надежд».

Я лишь могу предложить почитать эту книгу, которая дарит нам эту музыку любви, мечты, переживаний и надежд.

БРАВО, МЕГАН! ИЛИ МУДРОСТЬ ИЗМЕРЯЕТСЯ НЕ ГОДАМИ

> Будущее принадлежит тем, кто верит в красоту своей мечты.
>
> *Элеонора Рузвельт*

В свои 13 лет Меган Вернер написала книгу «Это зависит от меня. Семь способов изменить жизнь к лучшему», которая уже переиздана второй раз. Девочка из города Крюгесдорп Южной Африки учится в средней школе и мечтает о том, чтобы люди менялись к лучшему и сделали окружающий нас мир ещё прекрасней.

Когда читаешь таких авторов дидактических произведений, как Мишель Монтень, Ян Амос Коминский или Дейл Карнеги, ты невольно чувствуешь их жизненный опыт. Откуда у этой 13-летней девочки столько повседневной практики и мудрых умозаключений? Удивляешься не только тому, что написано ею, но и выражению мыслей.

Меган не умничает, она естественна и искренна. Любой тезис, приведённый в её книге, образно оживает примерами из собственных воспоминаний, прочитанных книг и личного опыта. Родители Меган и её сестра всегда рядом, и нередко именно они подсказывают ей, как найти правильный выход из сложившихся ситуаций и переменить эти ситуации к лучшему.

Десять глав книги – это прожитая жизнь девочки, описывающей запоминающиеся моменты. А названия глав можно использовать как крылатые выражения. Я не пою дифирамбы юному автору, а только выражаю свой читательский восторг. Приведу лишь несколько примеров, хотя вся книга написана таким не по годам мудрым и в то же время простым и понятным слогом.

Начинает Меган книгу словами благодарности, которыми пронизано всё повествование. Вот названия некоторых глав:

Делиться с ближними благородно
Никогда не прислушивайся к мнению пессимистов
Скажи мне, кто твой друг, и я скажу, кто ты

Книгу читаешь, как сборник ненавязчивых и заумных, а жизненных изречений, как будто ты это сам сказал или где-то слышал:

Ищите причины улыбаться каждый день,
даже если это порой кажется сложным.
Не зацикливайтесь на негативе.
Очень важно иметь пример для подражания:
Вы будете стремиться к идеалу,
и вдохновение Вас не покинет.
Будущее принадлежит тем,
кто верит в красоту своей мечты.

Мы должны научиться использовать

наши дары и таланты,

делиться ими с другими.

Если даже Вы устали от неудач, не сдавайтесь!

Будьте неординарными настолько,

насколько сможете.

Вы растёте только тогда,

когда находитесь вне зоны комфорта.

Это не просто короткие фразы и изречения: всё показано на примерах из жизни девочки-автора. Повествование также включает в себя истории из жизни современников, легенды предков.

И что же это за семь способов изменить жизнь к лучшему, которые предлагает Меган? Приведу ответы короткими тезисами, которые почерпнула из её книги:

1. Эффект отражения. Улыбнитесь, и мир улыбнётся Вам!

2. Чувство удовлетворения. Положительная энергия заразительна.

Не позволяйте печали из прошлого и страху о будущем разрушить счастье настоящего.

3. Мужество. (Здесь Меган внутри повествования приводит высказывание любимого Нельсона Манделы: «Я понял, что мужество – это не отсутствие страха, а победа над ним»).

4. Саморазвитие и самообразование – это прекрасный способ изменить к лучшему свою жизнь и жизнь других людей.

5. Обучение других: дай человеку рыбу, и он будет сыт один день, научи его ловить рыбу, и он будет сыт всегда.

6. Любовь к ближнему. Один человек не может изменить мир, но каждый может попробовать.

7. Научиться слушать и быть благодарным. Если Вы благодарны жизни за мелочи, вскоре Вы получите намного больше. Главное – идти по жизни с чувством благодарности.

Меган Вернер не заканчивает книгу. Она очень хочет встретиться со своими читателями в скорейшем будущем. И приводит красивый рассказ:

«Один старый китаец, который жил в горах, был известен своей мудростью. Люди со всего мира приезжали к нему за советом.

Однажды один подросток решил искусить старика. Он поймал бабочку. У него был план: придя с живой бабочкой в руках спросить у старца – жива она или мертва. Если старец ответит – «жива», он раздавит бабочку, а если ответит «мертва», то даст бабочке выпорхнуть.

– Господин, бабочка, которая у меня в руке – жива или мертва? – спросил он у старца.

После паузы старец сказал:

– Ответ лишь в твоих руках, мой сын».

И это действительно так, когда речь идёт о нашей жизни.

Меган Вернер не прощается с читателями. Она завершает свою книгу словами:

«До тех пор, пока мы не встретимся вновь, друзья, продолжайте менять жизнь к лучшему!»

Я советую всем прочитать эту книгу. Иногда мысли детей поражают нас, взрослых, своей наивной мудростью. А мудрость делает людей духовно богаче.

БЕЗМОЛВНО ПЛАЧА, ПРОСИТ БОГА...

Отзыв на книгу «Журавушка» Абу-Суфьяна

Только мать может так молиться за детей. Слова дагестанского поэта Абу-Суфьяна мне очень близки – он тоже дитя гор с восточным темпераментом и пишет на русском. Меня тронуло его отношение к маме, всё согласно канонам Священной книги «Ищите рай под ногами матерей».

Поэт рассказывает о жизни и не поучает читателей. Он делится с нами умением любить природу-мать, относиться бережно к близким, к тем, кого приручил.

Мне особенно понравились три стихотворных повествования: «Журавушка», «Кобылица» и современная баллада «Мама». Мы чувствуем в них боль автора, его переживания через истории матери-журавушки, матери-кобылицы. И их «судьбы» перекликаются с судьбами женщин-матерей, которые «живут, детьми забытые, одни». Автор даже называет свою журавушку нежным женским именем Роза. Эта сильная красивая птица не оставляет своего единственного сына, борется за его жизнь и побеждает:

Полетели, крыльями махая,
Роза с журавлёнком наконец...

Пусть их неудача никакая
Не постигнет больше, о Творец!

Кобылица ценой своей жизни спасает жеребёнка от жажды. Она сделала всё для продолжения своего рода. На это способна лишь мать:

Дорога дальняя пылится,
Бежит по ней не кобылица –
Бежит осиротелый жеребёнок.
И путь его под солнцем долог.
Очень долог...

Молитвы матерей всегда направлены на благополучие детей, даже тех, кто оставил их в старости. Мамы ждут своих кровиночек всегда:

И дни свои так коротая,
В плену мечтаний находясь,
Она сидит одна, слепая,
Утратив с белым светом связь.

Взрослому ребёнку тоже необходимо мамино моленье, хотя «уехал сын далёко, легко покинув дом родной». Она, обиженная судьбой, всё же надеется на его возвращение, глотает слёзы и

Безмолвно плача, просит Бога,
Чтоб сына Он хранил от бед...

Абу-Суфьян – поэт большого дарования и таланта. Стихи его написаны и для детей, и для взрослых. Я вижу в них много параллелей с притчами средневековой классической таджикско-персидской литературы. В образах птиц и животных легко узнаются характерные черты людей. Стихи поэта познавательны и поучительны. В них преобладает дух мудрости Востока.